CONTENTS

CHAPTER 4: KNOWLEDGE AND UNDERSTANDING OF THE WORLD

CHAPTER 5: PHYSICAL DEVELOPMENT

   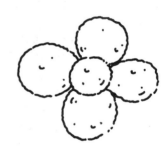

CHAPTER 6: CREATIVE DEVELOPMENT

PHOTOCOPIABLES

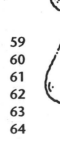 

LEARNING THROUGH PLAY

Clay & dough

LYNNE BURGESS

Published by Scholastic Ltd,
Villiers House,
Clarendon Avenue,
Leamington Spa,
Warwickshire CV32 5PR
Text © Lynne Burgess
© 1996 Scholastic Ltd
3 4 5 6 7 8 9 0   7 8 9 0 1 2 3 4 5

Author
Lynne Burgess

Editor
Jane Bishop

Assistant Editor
Sally Gray

Series designer
Lynne Joesbury

Designer
Clare Brewer

Illustrations
Angie Sage

Cover photograph
Fiona Pragoff

Designed using Aldus Pagemaker
Printed in Great Britain by Hartnolls Ltd,
Bodmin

British Library Cataloguing-in-Publication Data
A catalogue record for this book is available from the British Library.

ISBN 0-590-53638-9

INTRODUCTION

For young children, the sense of touch is an important means of exploring the world. Observe any young child meeting an object for the first time, and their natural response is to touch, stroke and feel it. Providing clay, play dough and Plasticine as a regular activity will extend their 'tactile' understanding. It will also offer new and different challenges with working in three dimensions.

Exploring the material

Although clay, play dough and Plasticine share many similarities, they also have some differences. Ideally, young children should handle all three so they can compare and contrast these 'plastic' materials.

Clay

When joining clay, use 'slip' which is made by adding a small amount of water to a piece of clay and mixing it to a double-cream consistency. It can then be applied with a brush. When joining modelling materials teach the children to seal the edges well by smoothing over the join with their fingers or a modelling tool.

If an activity involves rolling clay out, it is best to cover the table with hessian (or any other textured cloth) to prevent it sticking.

As children work, their hands become hot and sometimes the modelling material begins to dry out. Discourage children from adding extra water because the material can quickly become too wet and difficult to manipulate. Instead, offer the children a damp sponge to moisten their fingers.

Clay can be left to air dry over several days. The time required will depend upon the temperature and humidity of the environment and the thickness of the object. If the finished objects are to be handled a great deal, it is better to make them more durable by heating. Clay must be air dried for at least a week (to prevent breakages) and then fired in a kiln according to the manufacturer's instructions because different clays have different firing temperatures.

Real clay has a unique texture and it is important for children to experience this material. There are many different types of clay (earthenware, stoneware) and it is important to read the manufacturer's instructions for firing temperatures and appropriate glazes. Although clay objects can be air dried, it is valuable for children to witness the whole process of making, firing and glazing. If you do not have a kiln, try asking a local potter, secondary school or further education establishment. Alternatively, instructions for making and firing a sawdust kiln are given on page 27.

Clay objects which have been air dried or once (biscuit) fired can be painted with water-based paints and then varnished with PVA adhesive diluted with water (approximately two parts PVA to one part water). Biscuit fired objects can also be glazed by dipping, pouring or painting. Any glaze on the bottom of objects should be wiped off before refiring to prevent the object sticking to the kiln shelf.

Play dough

Traditional salt (play) dough is made with a simple salt, flour and water recipe (see page 36). Some people add a tablespoon of cooking oil for a smoother blend whilst others add two tablespoons of wallpaper paste to improve elasticity. As a rule, use plain white flour but you can experiment with other types such as wholemeal (which gives a texture) or self-raising (which is more elastic but will puff up when baked). A recipe for use with cornflour is given on page 34. You can vary colour with different food colourings or powder paints but remember the colours fade when baked or air dried so always make the dough a shade darker than you want. You can also add perfume with herbs or scented materials (such as perfume and talcum powder) or change the texture by including small amounts of sand, sawdust or oats.

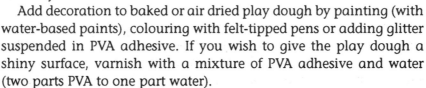

When joining play dough, use dough paste which is made by adding water to a small piece of dough and mixing until it resembles single cream. Make sure the dough paste is the same colour as the pieces to be joined. Play dough can be rolled out directly onto formica and a little extra flour sprinkled on the surface will prevent sticking. Play dough can be air dried or baked in an oven at 150°C (300°F, Gas mark 2) and on average this will take from three to four hours depending on the thickness of the objects. To check if the dough is adequately baked, tap the base. A hollow sound means the dough is cooked. Although fired clay and baked play dough objects are less fragile, the children will still need to handle them carefully.

Add decoration to baked or air dried play dough by painting (with water-based paints), colouring with felt-tipped pens or adding glitter suspended in PVA adhesive. If you wish to give the play dough a shiny surface, varnish with a mixture of PVA adhesive and water (two parts PVA to one part water).

Take care when you display the finished play dough objects. Too much heat may cause the objects to crack and they will absorb moisture in a damp environment.

Plasticine

Plasticine (a mixture of dry clay and mineral grease) is available commercially in many colours. Any Plasticine stains on work surfaces can be cleaned by white spirit but remember to keep the white spirit and any cleaning rags away from children. Work in Plasticine does not need any heating or special decoration.

Other modelling materials

There are also many other types of modelling materials available from educational suppliers. Some of the air dried clays can be painted (such as Model Magic, Crayola) and others are ready coloured (such as Modair, Specialist Crafts). There are also coloured clays which can be baked in an oven (such as Soffmo, NES). All these materials have a slightly different texture and it is useful for young children to experience some of them.

For each of the activities in this book, a specific modelling material has been suggested. However, it is often possible to substitute another modelling material with equal success.

Learning through play
Free play is vital when children are first introduced to modelling materials, in order to develop an understanding of the characteristics of materials and tools. These materials should be viewed as a 'tactile' experience as well as a means of producing objects. The process of exploring the material in more open-ended activities (such as Slap, bang, shake! on page 45 and Squeezing play dough on page 47) is as important as making specific objects. This book aims to extend children's play activities and to prompt them to investigate the endless possibilities inherent in these versatile materials.

Setting up the environment
Obviously, it is wise to keep any modelling activity well away from carpeted areas and minimise mess by providing aprons. If possible, the children can work directly onto formica or wooden tables. If this is not possible, cover the table with polythene sheeting and use base boards. Wooden base boards are better for clay whereas formica boards are more suitable for play dough and Plasticine.

In addition to specialist modelling tools, make a collection of everyday objects which can be used for modelling. These can include lollipop sticks, matchsticks, balsa wood, plastic knives and spoons. Also collect objects for creating textures, these can be natural objects (such as leaves, shells, sticks and stones) or man-made objects (such as a potato masher, keys, string, fabric and textured wallpaper). Shaped pastry cutters can be supplemented with plastic lids of different shapes and sizes.

Storage
Young children can become discouraged and frustrated if modelling materials are too hard or too soft to manipulate easily so correct storage is essential. Store all modelling materials in separate colours in airtight containers to prevent them drying out. If they do dry out, most materials can be reconstituted by wrapping in damp cloths and then kneading. The exception to this is Plasticine which should be softened in warm water, dried and kneaded.

Avoid storing Plasticine in a cold place because it becomes hard and brittle. On the other hand, home-made play dough keeps longer if stored in the fridge. Unfinished clay or dough work should be stored in polythene bags to prevent it drying out.

Health and safety

Make sure children always wear protective aprons when working with modelling materials. Check to make sure any modelling materials are non-toxic and that any glazes used contain safe ingredients. Discourage the children from putting their fingers in their mouths and always make sure they wash their hands thoroughly after handling any modelling material or glaze. Check with parents before using any modelling materials to see whether any children have allergies. Also, as the children use any new material, watch for any allergic reaction on their hands.

Don't contaminate modelling materials with foreign objects especially materials such as clay and play dough which are going to be heated in kilns or ovens. Always keep children well away from hot ovens and kilns.

Some modelling materials (especially play dough) look very appetising so always remind children not to try to eat any of the models. A CARE! warning has been added to each activity where particular caution is needed.

Dust from clay is a health hazard so always discourage children from any activity which creates excessive dust and keep work surfaces, floors, equipment and tools clean. Similarly, make sure all aprons are washed regularly.

Using adult helpers

Adult supervision can greatly enhance activities by stimulating discussion and promoting language development. Make sure adult helpers encourage the children to develop their own ideas. Being too prescriptive can limit the children's progress and hinder their discovery of each material's potential.

Observation and assessment

Working directly with a group of children will enable you to observe and assess each child's progress. Consider in your assessment: enthusiasm; perseverance; co-operation; confidence in using tools and materials; ability to learn and use appropriate vocabulary; willingness to experiment; confidence to develop their own ideas rather than copy others and the ability to talk about and evaluate any end product.

Links with home

Encourage parents and carers to become involved with the work you are doing. They may be willing to make play dough or help children gather objects for collections. Some may work with clay or dough (bricklayer, potter, sculptor, baker) and be willing to talk to the children about their job or hobby. Invite carers to view any displays of the children's finished work.

How to use this book

Chapters in this book are organised into the six Areas of Learning identified for under-fives by the School Curriculum and Assessment Authority. These are Language and Literacy (Chapter 1), Mathematics (Chapter 2), Personal and Social Development (Chapter 3), Knowledge and Understanding of the World (Chapter 4), Physical Development (Chapter 5) and Creative Development (Chapter 6).

Each activity begins with the learning objective identified and the ideal group size stated. Often an activity will be introduced to a whole group and then children will work in smaller groups on the task. The more adult helpers you have available will also influence the group sizes with which you work. A list of materials and equipment needed before the activity can begin is provided and any setting up procedures are identified.

Step–by–step instructions are outlined on how to introduce the activity and guidance is offered on what the children should do. The subsequent section provides suitable questions which you can ask the children either as they work or afterwards. It is best to adopt a flexible approach however and allow the children to lead the conversation into other, equally valid areas. Some activities may involve adult intervention throughout, while others may lend themselves to a summary discussion after the children have completed the task. Whenever possible, encourage the children to discuss ideas with a friend, an older child or an adult helper, as well as yourself.

Ideas for simplifying the task for younger children and ways of extending it for older children are given and finally some follow up activities are offered some which reinforce the main activity while others show cross-curricular links. In addition be prepared to follow up any idea suggested by the children.

Six photocopiable pages are included at the end of the book, each page links with a specific activity detailed earlier in the book. Make sure that the children understand how to do each sheet and that any new vocabulary is explained. Also allow time to discuss the completed sheet with each child in order to find out how much they have understood. The following page contains a photocopiable web showing all the activities in the book and their page references.

CLAY & DOUGH

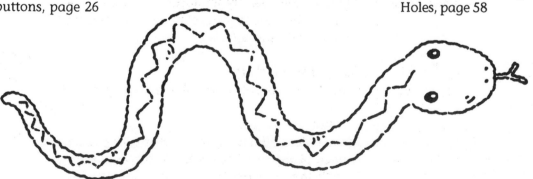

LANGUAGE AND LITERACY

These activities provide ways of using clay, play dough and Plasticine in order to help develop children's language and literacy skills. Some of the activities extend talking and listening skills whilst others support stories, rhymes and role-play.

SEASIDE STORY

Learning objective
To sequence a picture story.

Group size
Up to four children.

What you need
Photocopiable activity sheet on page 59, different coloured Plasticine, modelling tools, plastic wallets, pictures of seaside scenes.

Setting up
Make 12 photocopies of the activity sheet. Place each sheet inside a plastic wallet for protection.

What to do
Give three copies of the activity sheet to each child. Help the children to notice that their three sheets are all the same. Talk about the seaside picture on the sheet, and ask the children to suggest what else they might see at the seaside. Show them the other seaside pictures you have to extend their ideas.

Invite the children to make a story sequence about the seaside using their three activity sheets. Suggest that they make a Plasticine picture on top of each activity sheet. Some children will make flat images to press onto the sheet whilst more mature children may be able to make three-dimensional models such as boats and people.

When the children have finished their sequences, ask each child to show and tell their story to the rest of the group. Muddle up the three pictures and ask another child to order them correctly.

Questions to ask
Talk with the children about their pictures. What colour Plasticine will they choose to make their boat? Where will they place their Plasticine sun? Can they use the modelling tools to make textures or patterns on their pictures?

Encourage the children to talk about what is happening in each picture. Compare the pictures and identify similarities and differences. How would the story develop if they each had more activity sheets?

For younger children
Limit the number of activity sheets to two per child.

For older children
Invite older children to write what is happening in each picture on three separate pieces of paper. Muddle the pieces and ask the child to match them to the correct picture.

Follow-up activities
● Make a seaside scene in the sand tray.
● Set up a display of seaside items.
● Collect postcards from seaside resorts. Design and write your own.
● Mime a visit to the seaside. Include the journey, unpacking, playing on the beach, swimming in the sea, having a picnic.
● Provide towels of different sizes and ask the children to compare them and place them in size order.

CLAY WORDS

What you need
Clay, water, rolling pin, three shallow containers, three labels, three large pieces of paper, three different coloured felt-tipped pens.

Setting up
Divide the clay into three pieces. Roll one piece flat, allow it to dry out completely and then place it in one of the containers. Place the second piece of clay into a container in its original state. Place the third piece of clay into the last container and add water until it is very wet and sticky. Label each container using different coloured felt-tipped pens and different numbers – 1, 2 and 3. Then label each large piece of paper with the corresponding number in the relevant colour.

What to do
Ask each child to take turns to touch and explore each piece of clay, starting with the dry, then the medium and finally the wet clay. As each child handles the clay, ask them to think of words to describe it. Write the words in lists on to the corresponding pieces of paper.

Questions to ask
Encourage the children to use all their senses (apart from taste) to investigate each piece of clay. How does it feel? Can they make marks in it with their fingers? Will it bend or hold another shape? What colour is it? Can they make any sounds with it? Do the three samples smell differently? Talk about the reasons for not tasting the clay.

Look at the collection of words which the children have suggested. Do any appear in all three lists? Which is their favourite word and why?

For younger children.
Display the containers of clay with the number concealed and ask the children to match each list of words to the correct container.

For older children
Older children may be able to use the words from one list to make a short poem. They can either work individually or as a group with an adult acting as scribe.

FINGER PUPPET

Learning objective
To make a play dough finger puppet to stimulate conversation.

Group size
Up to four children.

What you need
Coloured play dough, dough paste, paintbrush for paste, modelling tools, baseboards.

What to do
Explain to the children that they are each going to make a finger puppet from play dough. Give each child a small piece of play dough and ask them to shape it into a sphere (to form a head). Show them how to roll it on their baseboard and then how to smooth out any cracks by using their fingers.

Suggest they make facial features such as a nose and ears by squeezing out with their fingers. Then encourage them to use the modelling tools to create eyes, mouth, hair and so on.

Ask them to decide which finger they want their puppet to fit onto and then help them gently press that finger into the bottom of their sphere. Make sure they don't push their finger all the way through the sphere. Remember that the play dough may shrink slightly when it dries, so avoid too tight a fit on the finger.

Allow the play dough finger puppet to harden by air drying before using. When the finger puppets are completely dry invite each child to use their puppet to have a conversation with either another child or an adult.

Questions to ask
As they work, encourage the children to talk about the character of their finger puppet. Is it male or female? Will it have large or small ears? What shaped nose would look best? Is it happy or sad? What kind of voice will it have? During the 'conversation' time, ask questions about how the puppet feels, where it lives, what it likes to eat or play.

Follow-up activities
● Reinforce positional vocabulary. Sing 'Tommy Thumb' but change the last line 'How do you do?' to a position such as 'behind my ear' or 'up on my head'. Can the children place their puppets in the correct positions?
● Make up a group short story about a finger puppet, with you scribing the children's ideas.
● Make an animal puppet by placing a ball of clay over a wooden or plastic spoon.
● Collect and use finger puppets made from other materials.

For younger children
Let younger children use simple methods to make their puppets using their fingers to squeeze out features and using tools to scratch in eyes, hair and so on.

For older children
Older children may be able to attempt more difficult methods of constructions such as joining pieces of dough with dough paste (see page 6). They may wish to add more details such as hair, eyebrows or a hat.

TOUCH ALPHABET

What you need
Plain play dough, baseboards, three rolling pins, six plastic knives, dough paste, paintbrush for the dough paste, plastic/wooden/card templates of lower case alphabet, modelling tools, non-stick baking sheet, oven, paints, paintbrushes, PVA adhesive and brushes.

What to do
Give each child a piece of play dough to make a backing tile. Ask them to roll it out about 5mm thick and large enough to place on a template-sized letter, with a border. Smooth the surface with fingers or modelling tools.

Give each child a second piece of play dough to roll out about 5mm thick again. Lay the chosen letter template on the play dough and with adult supervision let the child cut round it with a knife. Paint a little dough paste onto the backing tile and transfer the letter on to it. Press the letter firmly but gently into place. Ask the children to use the modelling tools to cut out the backing tile to an interesting shape and then add a texture or pattern.

Place all the alphabet tiles onto a baking sheet and bake in the oven at 150°C, (300°F, Gas mark 2) for three to four hours. Allow them to cool completely and then paint. Avoid too thick a layer of paint otherwise any textures will be lost.

Use the finished Touch Alphabet for a game. Blindfold a child and ask them to recognise and say the sound of a letter by touch alone.

Questions to ask
Can the children think of words beginning with the letter they have chosen. What distinguishing shapes is it made out of? Encourage them to feel and trace over their letter with their fingers, using the correct letter formation.

Compare and contrast the play dough before and after baking. What changes in size, shape, colour and hardness can be observed? Ask the children to describe any textures, patterns or colours which they use to decorate their tile.

For younger children
Instead of adding a raised letter, younger children could press the template into the play dough to form an impressed letter. They could also use ready-coloured play dough rather than painting the finished letter.

For older children
Older children may like to give their finished tile a slight shine by varnishing it with neat PVA adhesive.

PICNIC BASKETS

Learning objective
To respond to a story by making Plasticine models.

Group size
Up to six children.

What you need
A copy of *The Lighthouse Keeper's Lunch* by Ronda and David Armitage (Oliver & Boyd), coloured Plasticine, base board, modelling tools.

Setting up
Read the story to the children. Each day, Mrs Grinling makes a picnic basket lunch for her husband who is the lighthouse keeper. She sends it down a wire from her cottage to the lighthouse but the seagulls steal the food. Only mustard sandwiches eventually foil the thieves! Focus the children's attention particularly on the contents of the picnic basket.

What to do
Explain that the children are going to use Plasticine to make a picnic basket with food and drink. They can either invent their own food or make some depicted in the story. Refer them back to the pictures in the book for ideas.

Allow each child to choose the colour of their Plasticine, and suggest that they make a sphere (ball) shape and then hollow and squeeze it out to form the basket. Roll a thick cylinder shape and fix as a handle. Let the children make different foods to put in the basket. Display the finished baskets on individual paper tablecloths (see Follow-up activities).

Questions to ask
See how many of the foods from the story the children can remember. Make this into a game by asking a child to say 'In Mr Grinling's basket, there was...' and naming one food. Then suggest each child takes turns to repeat the previous list and then add one more food of their own. Talk with the children about the kinds of food and drink they want to put into their basket. Discuss including healthy foods such as fruit and vegetables.

For younger children
If younger children find making a basket too difficult, stick a cardboard handle onto a small plastic container (such as a yoghurt, margarine or cottage cheese pot) and cover the outside with paper.

For older children
Older children may want to make more difficult items such as cups, plates, knives and forks to include in their basket.

Follow-up activities
● Design and make simple tablecloths. Cut an interesting edge around a piece of coloured paper and then colour or stick patterns onto it.
● Make Plasticine seagulls and add to the display.
● Ask each child to empty their baskets and describe each food.
● Count the number of items in each basket and, if appropriate, sort them into sets such as sandwiches, cakes, fruit and vegetables.
● Make model lighthouses or cottages for Mr and Mrs Grinling.

BAKER'S SHOP

Learning objective
To make play dough
models to support role
play.

Group size
Up to six children.

What you need
Large piece of paper, felt-tipped pen, role-play area, small tables and shelves, till, money, purses, shopping bags, aprons and hats for the sales assistants, paper/plastic plates, cake stands/boards, small baskets, small cardboard boxes, plain and coloured play dough, dough paste, rolling pins, biscuit cutters, pictures of different breads, paper cake-cases, non-stick baking sheets, oven.

Setting up
Visit a baker's shop together and take photographs to inspire the role-play area. Talk with the children about what they want to include in their baker's shop. List their ideas. Tick each item as it is added to the shop.

What to do
Use the play dough to make a variety of breads, biscuits and cakes for the shop. Use rolling pins and different shaped cutters to make biscuits. Show the children pictures of different types of bread (pitta, brioche, croissant, bagel, bloomer) to inspire their models. Give the children paper cake cases to make cakes with currants, cherries or icing.

Air dry any cakes made over plastic pots but bake the others. Place onto a baking sheet and bake at 150°C, (300°F, Gas mark 2) for three to four hours. Display the finished food on plates, in baskets or boxes. Ask the children to buy and sell items in the shop. Have a bakery area beside the shop where food can be made.

CARE! Remind the children not to eat any of the play dough food.

Questions to ask
Talk about the size, shape, texture and decoration. What shape were the biscuits? Did the cakes have any decoration on the top? What patterns were on the different breads? Discuss how to display their models – singly on a cakestand, as a group in a basket or packaged in a box.

For younger children
Some children may need help understanding the role of the shop keeper or customer, handling money and developing appropriate vocabulary and will benefit from adult help in the role-play area.

For older children
Help individual children to write shopping lists based on items in the baker's shop. More mature children could also record the price of each item in the shop.

Follow-up activities
● Write and decorate signs, posters and labels for the shop.
● Make a collage of pictures of cakes, biscuits and breads cut from magazines.
● Design and make paper bags to use in the shop.
● Read *The Elephant and the Bad Baby* by Elfrida Vipont (Penguin).
● Make a birthday cake out of playdough: turn a plastic pot upside down, cover the sides and top with playdough. Add playdough candles, an age badge and other decorations.

THE GINGERBREAD MAN

Learning objective
To make a model to
accompany a story.

Group size
Up to six children.

What you need
A simple version of *The Gingerbread Man* (such as *The Gingerbread Man* (Favourite Tales Series, Ladybird Books), paper, pencils, crayons, card, stapler, thin coloured ribbon, clay, slip, hessian, wooden baseboard, modelling tools, rolling pins, a kiln, hole puncher, adhesive tape.

Setting up
Read the story to the children and sequence the main events. They can make individual books by drawing and writing the main events on separate pieces of paper. An adult can act as scribe for younger children. On each page tell the children to leave out the gingerbread man as they are going to make a clay model instead. Design a cover on card and staple the story pages inside.

What to do
To make a small clay gingerbread man, ask each child to roll out a piece of clay on the hessian about 1–2cm thick. Use the modelling tools to lightly draw an outline of a gingerbread man onto the clay. Cut round the outside of the figure with a modelling tool. Add eyes, hair and clothing to the outlines by pressing tools into the clay or adding small pieces of clay. When finished, pierce a hole through the top of each model and place onto a wooden baseboard (an adult will need to do this). Allow the models to dry and then fire them in a kiln.

Once fired, thread a piece of ribbon through the hole in the gingerbread man and through a hole punched in the top of each book. Tie the gingerbread man firmly to the book. Cut a card pocket corresponding to the size of the gingerbread man and tape it either to the front of the book or inside the front cover. The gingerbread man can now be moved through the story as they read and returned to the pocket.

Questions to ask
Talk about the features the children want to include on their gingerbread man. Will he have long or short hair? What clothing will he wear? Compare and describe the clay at various stages in the process. How has the clay changed from rolling it out, drying out on the baseboard to after firing.

For younger children
Younger children could use a gingerbread man shaped cutter to make the outline on the clay.

For older children
They can paint their finished gingerbread man with a glaze and refire it.

Follow-up activities
● Help individuals to read and show their completed book to a small group of children.
● Use the story to inspire dance and drama.
● Make gingerbread biscuits.
● Play the gingerbread man shape game on photocopiable page 60. Give each child a copy of the sheet and ask them to take turns to throw the shape dice and colour the matching shape. The winner is the first to colour all the shapes.

JACK-IN-THE-BOX

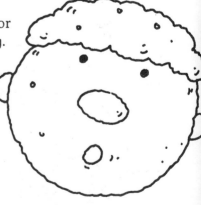

Learning objective
To make a model to
accompany an action
rhyme.

Group size
Up to six children.

What you need
A 'jack-in-the-box' action rhyme (as in *Gently into Music*
(Longman) or *Sing as You Grow* (Ward Lock Educational)),
plain play dough, dough paste, modelling tools, baseboards,
six lollipop sticks, non-stick baking tray, oven, felt-tipped
pens, six small plastic containers, coloured paper, PVA
adhesive, scissors, Stanley knife.

Setting up
Learn the rhyme.

What to do
Explain that the children are going to make a jack-in-the-box
to accompany the rhyme. To make the 'jack', give each child a
baseboard and a piece of play dough. Ask them to roll the play
dough into a sphere (ball) shape for a head. Suggest they add features
such as eyes, nose, mouth, ears and hair. Use the modelling tools to
add patterns and textures. Press a lollipop stick into the base of the
head and place on the baking tray. Bake at 150°C, (300°F, Gas
mark 2) for three to four hours. When completely cool, use
the felt-tipped pens to colour the hair, eyes and mouth or to
add freckles, wrinkles and glasses.
To make the box, give each child a plastic container and
ask them to decorate it by covering it with torn or cut pieces of
coloured paper. Encourage the children to stick the pieces flat
onto the outside of the container. When dry, assemble the jack-
in-the-box by cutting a slit in the base of the box with a Stanley
knife (an adult must do this). Slide the lollipop stick with the
'jack' into the slit and check to see it can move freely up and down.
Use the jack-in-the-box to accompany the rhyme.

Questions to ask
Talk about 'jack's' expression: will he be happy, sad or
surprised? Compare the play dough before and after cooking.
How has the colour or texture changed? Talk about the
decoration on the box. Will they cut or tear their pieces
of paper? Is each side of the box going to be the same?

For younger children
Encourage younger children to use simple methods of
construction, such as squeezing features out of the play dough
and using the modelling tools to scratch in eyes and hair.

For older children
Older children will be able to create features by adding pieces of play
dough. Remind them to use the dough paste to stick on ears, noses
and hair.

Follow-up activities
● Invite the children
to write stories about
their jack-in-the-
boxes. Do they like
living in a box?
● Make a collection
of toy jack-in-the-
boxes and discuss
how they work.
● Mime being jack-
in-the-box,
emphasising fast/
slow movements.
Jump up quickly and
curl up slowly and
vice versa.

CHAPTER TWO

Clay, play dough and Plasticine can all be used to add interest to practical mathematical activities. The following suggestions develop the children's knowledge of shape, size, matching, counting, pattern and shopping.

DINOSAURS

Learning objective
To compare length.

Group size
Up to six children.

What you need
Green play dough, photocopiable activity sheet on page 61, card, PVA adhesive, felt-tipped pens, plastic film, scissors.

Setting up
Photocopy one activity sheet per child. Stick each sheet onto card and colour the dinosaurs. Cover each card with plastic film and cut into three.

What to do
Give each child three dinosaur cards (one activity sheet). Talk about the dinosaurs: are they all the same size? Ask the children to point to the longest/shortest dinosaur. Explain that this type of dinosaur is called Diplodocus, which were the longest of the dinosaurs. They were vegetarian so they only ate plants such as leaves and stems.

Explain that the card dinosaurs will only eat stems which are the same length as their bodies. Show the children how to roll a cylinder shape with the play dough to represent a stem. Encourage them to use gentle even pressure with their fingers. Ask them to roll some stems for each dinosaur to eat, and to place each stem under the dinosaur which matches in length. Some children may also wish to decorate each stem with play dough leaves.

Remove the cards, muddle them up and ask each child to place the correct dinosaur above each set of stems.

Questions to ask
Encourage the children to use comparative vocabulary such as 'longer than', 'shorter than', 'longest', 'shortest' and 'as long as'. Make sure they measure correctly from the tip of the dinosaur's nose to the tip of his tail.

For younger children
Reduce the number of dinosaurs to two so they just compare 'long' and 'short'.

For older children
Repeat the task but ask the children to cut pieces of string or paper to match the length of each dinosaur.

Follow-up activities
● Make a collection of toy plastic dinosaurs. Make play dough stems to match the length of each one.
● Use information books to find out more about dinosaurs.
● Make an environment for plastic dinosaurs with reclaimed materials.
● Learn the song 'When a dinosaur's feeling hungry' in *Game-Songs with Prof Dogg's Troupe* (A & C Black).

SNAKES

Learning objective
To explore colour patterns.

Group size
Up to six children.

What you need
Different coloured play dough, dough paste, paintbrush for dough paste, modelling tools, baseboard, non-stick baking tray, oven.

What to do
Show the children how to roll a play dough snake approximately 25cm long and 2cm wide, shape a head and then use the modelling tools to make eyes and a mouth. Place the snake on a baseboard in a slightly curved shape. Choose two other different coloured play doughs and ask the children to make small balls with them. Paint a little dough paste along the length of the snake. Then invite one child to place the balls along the snake to form a colour pattern (red, blue, red, blue, for example). Ask the other children to check the pattern is correct before pressing the balls into the play dough snake.

Suggest that the children each make several snakes of their own and create their own two colour patterns. When finished, place the snakes on the baking tray and bake in the oven at 150°C (300°F, Gas mark 2) for three to four hours.

Questions to ask
Talk about the patterns, encouraging the children to point at and name each colour along the length of each snake. Does the pattern repeat correctly? If not, can they correct any mistakes? Suggest each child tries to make a different pattern on each of their snakes. Compare all the finished snakes and see whether any children have used the same patterns.

For younger children
Start the pattern on some snakes and ask the children to continue it.

For older children
Encourage older children to make snakes with more complex patterns using three colours.

Follow-up activities
● Display the snakes and ask the children to match any with the same colour patterns and ask them to copy one of the colour patterns onto a snake of their own.
● Use the photocopiable activity sheet on page 62, and ask the children to colour the circles to make a different colour pattern on each snake.
● Paint pictures of snakes with colour patterns on them.
● Collect pictures of snakes and describe the patterns on them.

SHAPING UP

Learning objective
To recognise plane shapes (square, circle, triangle, rectangle).

Group size
Up to six children.

What you need
Stories from the Mr Men series by Roger Hargreaves (World International) such as Mr Rush, Mr Happy, Mr Grumpy and Mr Strong, clay, wooden baseboard, rolling pins, hessian, objects/templates to make plane shapes, modelling tools, slip, a kiln.

Setting up
Read each story to the group and talk about each character's shape – Mr Rush is a triangle, Mr Happy is a circle, Mr Grumpy is a rectangle and Mr Strong is a square.

What to do
Explain that the children are going to make their own individual Mr Men out of clay. Give each child a piece of clay and ask them to roll it out on a piece of hessian until it is about 1–2cm thick. Suggest they choose an object or template for the shape they want (circle, square, rectangle, triangle). Place the object or template onto the clay, draw round it with a modelling tool and then cut it out. Transfer the shape to a wooden baseboard. An adult may need to help some children with the cutting and transferring.

Suggest the children add other features to their Mr Men. They could roll arms and legs or make clothing such as hats, belts and buttons. Make facial features by pressing or scratching into the clay with modelling tools or adding small pieces of clay (using slip as a glue). When complete, allow the models to dry thoroughly and then fire them in a kiln.

Questions to ask
Ask each child to name and talk about the shape they have chosen. How many edges does it have? Are they straight or curved? Encourage them to describe the shape of any other features they add to their Mr Men. What shape are the eyes, buttons or hat? Ask them to describe the character of their Mr Men. Is he happy, sad or angry? How does he behave? What does he enjoy doing?

For younger children
Younger children may need more help with rolling out and cutting the clay. If they are unfamiliar with plane shapes, offer them a choice between two rather than four shapes.

For older children
Suggest older children choose their Mr Men shape from a larger number of options. These could include hexagon, octagon, semi-circle.

Follow-up activities
● Ask each child to invent a name for their model and display the finished models with name labels.
● Write a joint zigzag book story about each character and add these to the display.
● Sort the models into sets according to the body plane shapes.
● Use the objects/templates to make a set of shapes in damp clay. Ask the children to match the objects/templates to the clay shapes.

MONKEY MODELS

Learning objective
To make models to accompany a counting song.

Group size
Up to five children.

Follow-up activities
● Place some monkeys on the bed and some beside it and count.
● Tie a numbered label around each monkey and place them in order on the bed.
● Create a display by building a complete bedroom for the monkeys.
● Mime the movements of monkeys such as jumping, climbing and swinging.
● Use information books to find out more about monkeys.

What you need
A copy of the song 'Five Little Monkeys', from *Okki-tokki-unga* (A & C Black), pictures of monkeys, plain play dough, baseboard, modelling tools, oven, felt-tipped pens, thin elastic, cuboid shaped box, card, fabric, scissors.

Setting up
Learn the song 'Five Little Monkeys'. Talk about the pictures of monkeys. What shape are they? Count the body parts such as ears and legs. Describe the colour and texture of their fur.

What to do
Explain that each child is going to make a monkey to accompany the song. Give each child a piece of play dough and ask them to shape it into a sphere (ball) shape. Place the play dough on the baseboard and squeeze out a head, ears, arms, legs and tail. Invite them to use the modelling tools to add features such as eyes, mouth and fur. Bake in an oven at 150°C (300F, Gas Mark 2) for three to four hours. When cool, use the felt-tipped pens to colour the monkeys. Tie a piece of elastic around each monkey.

Invite the children to change the cuboid shaped box into a bed. Add a card headboard and make a quilt and pillow from the fabric. As the children sing, ask them to hold the elastic and bounce their monkey on the bed.

Questions to ask
Throughout the activity, encourage the children to touch and count as much as possible. Can they count the number of baseboards, modelling tools and pieces of card? Count the physical characteristics on each monkey such as eyes, mouth and legs. Place the finished monkeys in a row and practise counting forwards to five and backwards to one.

For younger children
Very young children could start with a lower number of monkeys and build up to five.

For older children
Older children may be able to use a larger number of monkeys (up to ten).

ONE EACH

Learning objective
To match objects,
using one-to-one
correspondence.

Group size
Up to six children.

What you need
Six ice-cream carton lids, white card, scissors, felt-tipped pens, plastic film, small model people (Duplo, LEGO, Playmobil), coloured Plasticine.

Setting up
Cut six small pieces of white card (approximately 4cm × 4cm). On each card, draw and colour a small picture of something which the children could easily make from Plasticine (such as a ball, a bat, a skateboard, a hoop, a teddy and a boat). Seal a picture onto each plastic lid with the plastic film. On each lid place a different number of small model people.

What to do
Go through some examples together as a group. Show the children one plastic lid and ask them to identify the picture on it. Place four small model people on the lid and explain that each of these children want a ball (the picture). Ask one child to make a ball out of Plasticine for each model person and to place them next to each other on the lid. Ask the other children to check it has been done correctly. Once the children have grasped what to do, allow them to choose a lid and to make the correct number of relevant objects. Repeat as often as required, encouraging the children to check each other's work.

Questions to ask
As the children make and match their objects, ask the following questions. Are there enough balls for each model 'child'? Are there more balls or more children? Are there too many balls? How do you know?

For younger children
Use a smaller number of model people (up to five).

For older children
Use a larger number of model people (up to ten).

Follow-up activities
● Reinforce matching one-to-one during work with small apparatus. Ask children to give a bean bag or hoop to each child.
● Match a set of lids to a set of containers.
● Collect empty chocolate/biscuit trays. Ask the children to make Plasticine chocolates/biscuits for each empty space.

ICE-CREAM VAN

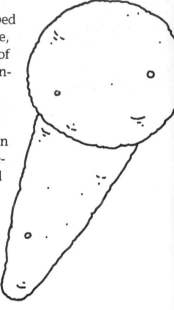

Learning objective
To make models for
role-play shopping
activities.

Group size
Up to six children.

What you need
Child-sized play truck, small ice-cream cartons, paper, felt-tipped pens, adhesive tape, plain and coloured play dough, dough paste, paintbrush for dough paste, shape cutters, pictures of a variety of ice-cream products, modelling tools, lolly sticks, baseboard, non-stick baking tray, oven, money, purses.

Setting up
If possible, visit an ice-cream van together. Next show the children the play truck and discuss how it could be changed into an ice-cream van. For example, empty ice-cream cartons could be used to hold the different ice-creams and signs could be stuck on the side of the truck. Talk about what the ice-cream seller should wear, and what could be used to hold the money?

What to do
If appropriate, remind the children of their visit to the ice-cream van. Talk about the pictures of the ice-creams and invite the children to use the play dough to make pretend ice-creams. These could include ice-cream cones (with different toppings – cherry, flake, chocolate chips), ice-lollies (different shapes and sizes), wafers and choc-ices. Suggest that the children use the modelling tools to add patterns or textures.

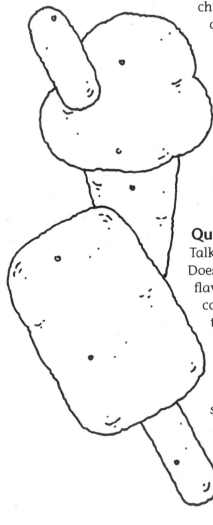

When complete, place the models onto a baking tray and bake in the oven at 150°C (300°F, Gas mark 2) for three to four hours. When cool, put the ice-creams in the cartons in the play truck. Encourage the children to role play buying and selling ice-creams.

CARE! Remind the children not to eat any of the models.

Questions to ask
Talk about the colour of the play dough the children choose. Does it represent a particular flavour? Which is their favourite flavour? Use the opportunity to reinforce solid shapes such as cones, spheres and cuboids. What pictures, patterns or textures will they put on their models? For example, can they make an ice-lolly with a monster face on it?

For younger children
Ask an adult to work with the children as the ice-cream seller. Give the customers some 1p coins which they can exchange for ice-creams priced up to 5p .

For older children
Older children could draw up a price list using amounts appropriate to their experience.

Follow-up activities
● Use chime bars to make up a 'jingle' for the ice-cream van.
● Make real ice-cream or flavoured ice-cubes.
● Use pictures to record the children's favourite flavour ice-cream.
● Read the story *Teddy Bears Go Shopping* by Suzanna Gretz (Hippo Books), in which the bears forget everything except the ice-cream.
● Challenge the children to make as many different shaped lollies as they can. Try heart shapes, faces and stars, what patterns can they make-up?

SALAD TALLY

What you need
Selection of four or five different salad foods (radishes, cucumber, tomatoes, carrots, lettuce), knife, large pieces of white paper, felt-tipped pens, coloured Plasticine, wooden baseboard, modelling tools.

Setting up
Show salad foods to the children and discuss the shape, colour, texture and smell of each one. Ask what part of the plant do we eat? Cut a small piece of each salad food for each child to taste. Talk about the taste and ask each child to say which of these salad foods they like best.

Draw a large picture of each salad food on a separate piece of paper. Label with the appropriate name.

What to do
Explain to the children that they are going to make a tally to record their favourite salad food from the selection tasted. Ask them to use the Plasticine on the baseboard to make a model of their favourite salad. Suggest they use the modelling tools to add textures or patterns. When they have finished, ask each child to place their model on top of the picture which matches their salad food.

Repeat this activity with one or two more groups. Then talk with all the children about the results of the tally. Compare and contrast the number of models on each picture. Encourage the children to compare two sets by placing the models in two lines and matching one-to-one.

Questions to ask
What colour Plasticine will they need? What shape is their fruit or vegetable? Does it have leaves, stem or roots? What patterns or textures are there? Encourage the children to make comparisons. Do more children like lettuce or carrots? How many more children like tomatoes than cucumber?

For younger children
Keep the number of models on each picture within the counting abilities of the children by restricting the number of children taking part in the tally.

For older children
Encourage the older children to make comparisons and articulate their conclusions using appropriate mathematical language, such as 'More people liked carrots than lettuce'. You may like to help them record their findings and display the results alongside the pictures and models.

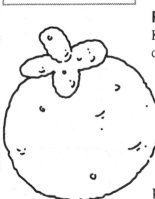

SNOWMAN BUTTONS

Learning objective
To reinforce counting up to five.

Group size
Up to four children.

What you need
White card, felt-tipped pens, scissors, plastic film, Plasticine, dice with three faces blank and three faces with five spots.

Setting up
Cut out 16 pieces (approximately A4 size) from the card. On each piece, draw and colour a large snowman (without buttons). Cut each snowman out and cover with plastic film to protect it.

What to do
Give each child four snowmen. Point out that each snowman needs five buttons. Ask the children to take turns to throw the dice. If five spots are shown the child makes five Plasticine buttons and places them on one snowman. If the dice shows a blank, no buttons are made and the dice is passed to the next player. Continue the game until one player has made buttons for each of their snowmen.

Questions to ask
Make sure the players touch each button (or spot on the dice) as they count. Encourage the children to use the word zero to describe the blank faces of the dice. During the game, pause to count how many snowmen have all their buttons and how many have none.

For younger children
Adjust the number of snowmen and the number of buttons to suit the counting ability and concentration span of the children involved. For example, younger children may be better making two buttons for three snowmen.

For older children
Change the dice to a one to six spot dice. The children can make the number of buttons shown on each dice throw and place them on the snowmen, carrying them over to the next snowman if there are more than is needed to complete one snowman. They must throw the exact number to complete the last snowman.

Follow-up activities
● Make a collection of buttons and sort them into sets.
● Challenge the children to do up as many buttons on garments as possible before the sand runs through an egg timer.
● Press buttons into play dough to make patterns or pictures.
● Thread buttons on to a lace to make a sequence.
● Write a group story about a child who has lost a button from a special piece of clothing.

CHAPTER THREE

Personal and Social Development is an important element of children's early learning. The following activities highlight areas such as co-operation with other people, hygiene and respect for materials and festivals.

DIWALI DIVAS

Learning objective
To make divas from clay.

Group size
Up to six children.

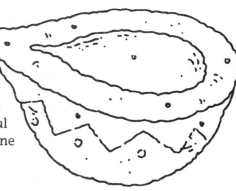

What you need
A simple version of the story of Rama and Sita (*Playtime Activity Book*, BBC and *Festivals*, *Teacher Timesavers* series, Scholastic), real divas, clay (Raku or any other low-firing clay), modelling tools, wooden baseboards, an old metal dustbin (with lid), sharp implement for making holes, fine sawdust, firelighter, six nightlights, matches.

Setting up
Read and discuss the story of Rama and Sita. If available, show and talk about the real divas and how they are used in the Hindu/Sikh festival of Diwali which falls in October or November.

What to do
Invite the children to make their own divas. Give each child a small lump of clay and ask them to roll it into a sphere (ball), smoothing any cracks with their fingers. Show them how to push their thumbs gently into the centre of the sphere and pinch the walls evenly, turning the sphere as they work. Flatten the bottom by tapping it gently on the baseboard and pinch a spout at one edge. Use the tools to scratch patterns on the outside of the diva, and leave them to dry thoroughly.

Make a sawdust kiln (right) to fire the divas. Remove the divas from the dustbin and wash them. Place a nightlight in each one, display and light them.

Follow-up activities
● Act out the story of Rama and Sita.
● Make food associated with Diwali such as samosas and pakora.
● Collect and observe candles of different shapes and sizes.
● Design and make a card for Diwali.

Questions to ask
Talk about how the firing process has changed the clay. Look for differences in colour, texture, size and hardness. If possible, compare and contrast the children's divas with a real diva. Assess how well the divas function and discuss any changes the children would make next time. When the divas are alight, have a time of quiet reflection and ask the children to describe their response to the candles.

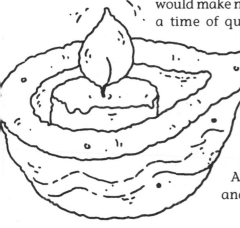

For younger children
Use airdrying clay instead of making a sawdust firing.

For older children
Ask older children to record the making and firing process.

Sawdust kiln
Find a sheltered site away from buildings and not accessible to the children. Punch holes approximately 1cm in diameter and at 15cm intervals into an old metal dustbin to allow ventilation for even burning. Place a 10cm layer of fine sawdust in the bottom of the dustbin and then stand the divas in the centre, leaving a 10cm gap at the edge. Cover the divas with sawdust (at least 8cm) and then repeat layers of divas and sawdust, finishing with a 15cm layer of sawdust at the top. Fire the kiln when it is not windy by lighting a firelighter on top of the sawdust so that it smoulders gently. Use the lid to control the draught by putting it on tightly if the sawdust is burning too quickly. It will probably smoulder for two days and should then cool naturally. The outside of the dustbin does become very hot, so make sure the children do not go near it during the firing process.

PICTURE PUZZLES

Learning objective
To make clay puzzles to be used co-operatively.

Group size
Up to six children.

What you need
A copy of *The Great Big Enormous Turnip* by A Tolstoy (Picture Lions), clay, slip, rolling pins, hessian, wooden baseboards, modelling tools, access to a kiln, two hoops.

Setting up
Read and discuss the story with the children. Point out that everybody had to co-operate to pull up the turnip.

What to do
Ask each child to roll a piece of clay on the hessian until it is approximately 1cm thick. Cut a square tile (20cm × 20cm) from the clay. An adult may need to do this. Ask the children to make a picture of some aspect of the story on their tile. Use the modelling tools to scratch a picture into the tile or create raised areas by adding clay, using slip to join pieces and sealing thoroughly. When complete ask each child to cut their tile into two pieces (using a simple curve) to make a puzzle. Allow the puzzle to dry thoroughly and then fire in a kiln.

Use the clay puzzles in a co-operative game. Muddle up the pieces and place them upside down in a hoop. Place an empty hoop a short distance away. Ask the children to work together to move the puzzle pieces from the first hoop and assemble them correctly in the second hoop.

Follow-up activities
● Act out the story.
● Work together to make a group picture of the final scene in the story where everyone is helping to pull up the turnip.
● Play other co-operative games. For example, ask two children to hold a balloon between them (head to head, or back to back) without using their hands. Can they move it a short distance?

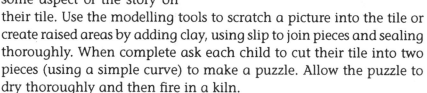

Questions to ask
As the children work, talk about how they are co-operating. For example, they may be sharing tools and equipment or taking turns to use the slip. Talk about how successful the co-operative game was. Were there any problems and how could these have been solved? Did everyone work together or did one person dominate?

For younger children
Reduce the number of pieces of puzzle in the co-operative game.

For older children
Play the co-operative game without talking. Can they find other ways of communicating?

DIRTY HANDS!

Learning objective
To reinforce the
importance of hygiene.

Group size
Up to six children.

What you need

Clay (wet and sticky), six pieces of white paper, six magnifying
glasses, washing up bowls, water, soap, nail brushes, sponges,
paper towels, felt-tipped pens.

Setting up

Allow the children sufficient time to play with the clay
so their hands are very dirty.

What to do

Give each child a piece of white paper and ask them to
find out how dirty their hands are. Suggest that they press
their hands flat onto the paper several times to make hand/
finger prints. Use magnifying glasses to examine their hands
in detail. Are they still dirty? Invite the children to wash their hands,
using the soap, sponges and nail brushes.
Dry their hands on the paper towels and
then use the magnifying glasses again to
observe and then describe their hands.

When the clay prints have dried, turn
them into posters by asking each child to
think of a hygiene message to put on their
paper. Display the finished posters and talk
about the messages.

Questions to ask

Talk about how the clay transfers from the
children's hands to the paper and ask them
to predict what would happen if they were
to eat food with similar dirty hands. Remind
them that whilst we can see dirt, our hands
are also often covered in germs which we
cannot see. Discuss the health implications.
Use the magnifying glasses to look for dirt hiding under their nails
and in cracks in their skin. Talk about the advantages of using soap,
sponges and nailbrushes and remind them to wash the backs of their
hands. Why are paper towels more hygienic
than fabric towel?

For younger children

An adult can act as scribe to help younger
children to write a message on their poster. They
could write over to decorate the adult's writing.

For older children

Invite older children to use the felt-tipped pens
to decorate or illustrate their poster further.

Follow-up activities
● Talk about the design of commercially
produced health education posters. How
successful are they?
● Play with a variety of soaps in the water
tray.
● Match pairs of soaps according to scent.
● List the occasions when you need to wash
your hands (before eating/after going to the
toilet/after a messy activity).
● Read the poem 'Mud' in *Twinkle, Twinkle
Chocolate Bar* (OUP).

ROW YOUR BOAT

Learning objective
To work co-operatively in a singing game.

Group size
Any size.

What you need
A copy of 'Row, row, row your boat', *This Little Puffin* (Young Puffin), a large space, play dough.

Setting up
Learn the song and accompanying actions. As they sing, the children sit opposite each other in pairs with knees bent, hold hands and sway forwards and backwards.

What to do
Give each pair of children a piece of play dough and ask them to roll it into a short fat rope. Invite them to sit as before but instead of holding hands, they each hold one end of the rope. The children repeat the song but must move together very carefully so they don't break the play dough rope. Repeat this activity several times, each time making the play dough rope slightly thinner.

Questions to ask
Talk about the importance of swaying gently together. What happens if the children don't move together? Which pair of children can make the thinnest rope without breaking it?

For younger children
Encourage the children to sing and move very slowly.

For older children
Encourage the children to sing and move more quickly.

Follow-up activities
● Play other singing games with actions for the whole group to do together such as 'Here We Go Looby Loo' or 'The Hokey Cokey'.
● Make play dough rowing boats for two toy plastic people.
● Build a large rowing boat from cardboard boxes.
● Collect different types of toy boat and discuss their similarities and differences.

EASTER EGGS

Learning objective
To make clay Easter eggs.

Group size
Up to five children.

What you need
Spot's First Easter by Eric Hill (Picture Puffin), clay, wooden baseboards, plastic knife, access to a kiln, paint, paintbrushes, palettes.

Setting up
Read the story, in which Spot and his friends search for Easter eggs hidden under flaps. Also talk about why we give eggs at Easter.

What to do
Give each child a baseboard and a piece of clay. Ask them to roll their clay into an egg shape on the baseboard, smoothing any cracks with their fingers. Flatten the bottom of the egg slightly by tapping it gently on the baseboard. Use the plastic knife to cut the top off the egg. Hollow out the bottom of the egg by inserting a thumb and squeezing the walls of the egg gently to thin them. Repeat with the top of the egg. Keep the rim of each half fairly thick. Smooth any rough edges inside with the fingers and make sure the lid and the base of the egg fit together. Allow the eggs to dry thoroughly and then fire in a kiln.

When the eggs are cool, glaze them if possible. If not, paint them with bright patterns such as stripes, zigzags and spots. Hide a toy chick inside each egg.

Questions to ask
Compare the changes between the raw and fired clay. How has the colour, size, shape and texture changed? Talk about the choice of colours the children use to decorate their eggs. Which is their favourite colour and why? Ask the children to describe their patterns. Do any of them repeat? What else could they hide in their eggs instead of chicks?

For younger children
An adult may need to help younger children hollow their egg.

For older children
Older children could make a chick to hide in their egg. Give them a choice of materials such as card, Plasticine, cotton wool or reclaimed materials.

Follow-up activities
● Play a guessing game. Hide a chick in one egg but have several others empty. The children guess where the chick is hiding.
● Collect egg cups and compare the different materials which they are made from.
● Have an egg hunt inside or outside.
● Make Easter-egg shaped Easter biscuits.

PLAY DOUGH RULES

Learning objective
To list the rules associated with the use of play dough.

Group size
Up to six children.

What you need
Large piece of paper, felt-tipped pen, plain and coloured play dough, dough paste, paintbrush for paste, modelling tools, straw, baseboards, rolling pins, display board covered in black backing paper, mapping pins, white paper cut into speech bubble shapes, stapler.

Setting up
Talk with the children about the rules which need to be followed when using play dough. Write each rule as a list on the large piece of paper. These might include – cover the table with a cloth, wear an apron, don't drop play dough on the floor, wash your hands afterwards, returned unused play dough to a container with a lid and wash any tools.

What to do
Ask the children to choose one of the rules from the list and write it onto the speech bubble shaped piece of paper. Then ask them to make a play dough picture of their face to go with their speech bubble.

To do this give each child a plain piece of play dough and ask them to roll it out about 1cm thick. Use a modelling tool to lightly draw a head shape and then cut it out. Place the head shape on the baseboard and add features to the face. Either press the modelling tools into the play dough or add pieces of coloured dough using the paste to stick. When the face is finished, use the straw to pierce two small holes near the top of the head. Allow the play dough faces to airdry. Create a display by using two mapping pins to secure each play dough face to the board. Staple the corresponding speech bubble beside each face and add a label 'When we use play dough, we must ...'.

Questions to ask
As the children work with the play dough, talk about the rules they are trying to follow. Which rules are most difficult to keep? Make sure the children understand the reason for each rule. What are the consequences if a rule is broken?

For younger children
An adult can act as scribe to help younger children to write in their speech bubble. They could write over or decorate the adult's writing.

For older children
Older children could write several rules in their speech bubble.

Follow-up activities
● Compare the rules followed for play dough with another area such as sand or water.
● Ask two or three children to act out playing with play dough. Include some examples of forgetting the rules for the audience to spot.
● Ask individual children to explain the rules for a simple game to the group. Discuss why it is important to follow the rules.

CHINESE NEW YEAR

Learning objective
To make models of
dragons for the
Chinese New Year.

Group size
Up to six children.

What you need
Pictures of dragons, clay, slip, wooden baseboards, modelling tools, paints, paintbrushes, palettes, toy plastic people.

Setting up
Talk with the children about the significance of the dragon in the Chinese New Year celebrations. Each New Year has the name of an animal and the dragon is the most important because it signifies a year of good fortune. On New Year's Eve, there is often a procession headed by a giant paper and silk dragon. People inside the dragon make it dance and rear up to get gifts which have been hung outside windows.

What to do
Look at the pictures of dragons and talk about their physical characteristics. Name and describe their body parts. Invite the children to make their own dragon. Ask each child to roll a piece of clay into a thick cylinder shape on the baseboard. Suggest they squeeze out legs, a head and a tail. Use slip to stick on other features such as eyes or wings. Seal any additions onto the body of the dragon. To create texture or patterns, press the modelling tools into the clay surface. Allow the finished dragons to airdry thoroughly and then paint them in bold colours and patterns. Display the dragons in a procession with toy plastic people following behind.

Questions to ask
Does the dragon have an open mouth with teeth? Is the tail long, short, straight or curved? Which areas of the dragon's body are bumpy or smooth? Point out the changes in the clay as it dries. Talk about the colours the children choose. Will the dragon be mainly one colour or lots of different colours? Can they paint spots or stripes on top of another colour?

For younger children
Younger children can use simple techniques such as pinching and squeezing rather than sticking on additional pieces of clay.

For older children
Make clay or Plasticine people to add to the dragon procession.

Follow-up activities
● Make a giant dragon. Use a box for the head and a sheet for the body. Invite children to wear the 'dragon' and make it dance.
● Use percussion instruments to accompany the dragon dance.
● Make 'Lucky Money Envelopes' which are traditionally given to children at Chinese New Year. Fold red paper to form an envelope and make 'money' by pressing coins into rolled out play dough.

CHRISTMAS STARS

Learning objective
To make stars as
Christmas decorations.

Group size
Up to six children.

What you need
125g cornflour, 250g salt, 350ml water, food colouring, saucepan, wooden spoon, hob, plastic chopping board, rolling pins, pastry cutters (different shapes and sizes, including star shapes), six thick straws, non-stick baking sheet, oven, PVA adhesive, water, glitter, brushes, shiny string, hoop covered in shiny paper.

Setting up
Make the cornflour dough. If time allows, invite the children to help. Place all the ingredients into the saucepan and mix thoroughly. Cook over a medium heat, stirring constantly until the mixture forms a ball. (An adult must heat the ingredients.) When thoroughly cooked, tip onto the plastic chopping board and leave to go cold. Talk to the children about any changes that occur to the ingredients.

What to do
Ask each child to knead a piece of cornflour dough to an even consistency. Roll it out until it is roughly ½cm thick. Then use the pastry cutters to cut shapes from the dough. Each shape must include a star either as the main shape or as a hole within another shape. Use a straw to pierce a hole in the top of each shape. Place the shapes on a baking tray and bake in the oven at 150°C (300°F, Gas mark 2) for one or two hours. When cold, paint one side of the shapes with a mixture of half PVA adhesive, half water and glitter. When dry, paint the other side. When completely dry, thread a string through the hole and suspend from a hoop to create a mobile.

Questions to ask
Describe the feel of the cornflour dough. Name the shapes of the pastry cutters and discuss their sizes. Compare the shapes before and after baking. Can the children predict how the heat will change the shapes? Contrast the PVA and glitter mixture before and after it dries. Talk about the finished mobile. What makes the stars move? What effect does the glitter have?

For younger children
An adult may need to help younger children pierce the hole with a straw and to thread and tie the shape to the mobile.

For older children
Suggest older children produce designs beforehand. They may draw round the pastry cutters on paper and experiment with different combinations, choosing some to make with the cornflour dough.

Follow-up activities
● Compare the cornflour dough with other types of play dough.
● Make star shapes using wooden or plastic mosaics.
● Talk about why stars are an important symbol at Christmas.
● Print Christmas cards with star pictures.
● Write a simple poem about stars.

CHAPTER FOUR

The activities in this chapter will help develop children's understanding of their environment and other people. Essential skills for future work in history, geography, science and technology are introduced.

FARMYARD JOURNEY

Learning objective
To use play dough models to represent a journey.

Group size
Up to four children.

What you need
Rosie's Walk by Pat Hutchins (Picture Puffin), different coloured play dough, modelling tools, a baseboard for each child.

Setting up
Read the story *Rosie's Walk* about a hen who goes for a walk around a farmyard. She is unaware that she is being followed by a fox who has all kinds of accidents along the way. Make sure the children are familiar with the objects and places Rosie passes on her journey around the farmyard.

What to do
Start by asking each child to make a small model hen from play dough. Then explain that they are going to make models of the important things that Rosie passed on her journey. Encourage them to use the modelling tools to add pattern and texture to their models. Suggest they refer to the story if necessary.

Ask the children to place each finished model on the baseboard to correspond with the order in the story. Then ask each child to walk their hen along the journey, naming the objects and places as they pass. Some children may like to make a model fox who could also be included in the journey.

Questions to ask
As the children talk, encourage them to use positional vocabulary such as 'on', 'around', 'beside' and 'behind'. When the children are very familiar with the journey sequence, muddle up the models. Can they spot the mistakes and correct them? Can they use the same models but invent a different route for Rosie to take?

For younger children
Let the children work together to each produce one object or place on the journey. They can then sequence the journey together.

For older children
Suggest the children use play dough to make their own imaginary journey for another bird or animal.

Follow-up activities
● Walk two or three different routes around the room and ask the children to name the objects or places which they pass.
● List the objects or places passed on a familiar journey such as to playgroup or nursery.
● Use the photocopiable activity sheet on page 63 and ask the children to find and colour the fox hidden in each picture.

MAKING PLAY DOUGH

Learning objective
To observe changes which occur when making play dough.

Group size
Up to four children.

What you need
Half-litre measuring jug, metal spoon, plain white flour, salt, water, food colouring, large mixing bowl, wooden spoon, modelling tools, six baseboards, non-stick baking tray, oven, plastic bag.

What to do
Ask one child to spoon half a litre of flour into the measuring jug and then tip it in to the mixing bowl. Invite a second child to half fill the jug with salt and add this to the flour. Take turns to mix the flour and salt together. Ask another child to half fill the jug with water and to add a little food colouring. Remember that the colour fades when play dough is baked or air dried. Gradually add this coloured water to the flour and salt. Take care not to add too much water otherwise the mixture will become too sticky.

Give each child a share of the play dough and show them how to knead it for about ten minutes into a pliable dough.

Using a small piece of dough and a baseboard, ask the children to make two models of their choice using their fingers and the modelling tools. Place one model on a baseboard to air dry and the other on the baking tray. Bake the second set of models for three to four hours at 150°C (300°F, Gas mark 2). Place any unused play dough in a plastic bag. Compare and contrast a piece of soft play dough with the baked and air dried models.

CARE! Make sure the children understand that play dough must not be eaten.

Questions to ask
Feel the salt and the flour and describe any differences. How does the coloured water change the flour and salt mixture? Look for similarities and differences between the soft play dough and the baked and air dried models. Is the colour the same on all three? Feel each example and describe any differences in texture. Tap each one gently and talk about any difference in sound.

For younger children
Ask younger children to describe how to make play dough. Can they remember the correct sequence of events?

For older children
Suggest older children draw and write the correct sequence of events for making play dough.

Follow-up activities
● Draw the sequence of events for making play dough on a series of cards. Muddle them up and ask individuals to order them correctly.
● Use sand and water with the measuring jug to reinforce 'full', 'half full' and 'empty'.
● Make cheese straws and compare the ingredients and method with making play dough.

FRAGRANT FLOWERS

Learning objective
To focus on the sense of smell.

Group size
Up to six children.

What you need
Coloured play dough, two different perfumes, baseboard, modelling tools, shape cutters, rolling pin, three sorting hoops.

Setting up
Show the children the two perfumes. Talk about the shape of the bottle, the colour and the name. Invite them to smell and describe each perfume. Ask what it makes them think of.

What to do
Divide the play dough into three pieces. Put the first to one side unperfumed. Make a small well in the middle of the second piece of play dough and pour on a little of the first perfume. Invite the children to take turns to knead the play dough until the perfume is well mixed in. Repeat with the third piece of play dough and the second perfume.

Ask each child to make one flower from each piece of play dough. Invite them to use a combination of fingers, modelling tools and shape cutters. When complete, muddle up the flowers and ask the children to sort them into the three sorting hoops according to smell.

Questions to ask
Which perfume do they like best/least? Does the perfume smell stronger in the bottle or in the play dough? Ask the children to name flowers which have a strong smell. Which ones do they like/dislike? Is it easy or difficult to sort the play dough flowers according to smell?

For younger children
Use one perfume only so the children are only having to distinguish between perfumed and unperfumed.

For older children
Ask older children to write a description of one of their flowers and how it smells.

Follow-up activities
● Invite the children to find other fragrant substances to mix with play dough. They could try coffee powder, spices, talcum powder and orange juice.
● Blindfold a child and ask them to recognise a range of different substances by smell alone.
● Collect fragrant plants and flowers.
● Ask children to make a list of smells which they like and dislike.
● Read *The Smelly Book* by Babette Cole (Picture Lions).

CLAY DISPLAY

Learning objective
To create a display of objects made from clay.

Group size
Any size.

What you need
Display board covered in dark blue backing paper, white paper, felt-tipped pens, scissors, three large cardboard boxes, dark blue fabric, objects/pictures of objects made from clay (such as bricks, tiles, chimney pot, flower pot, jug, cup, teapot, sculpture, ornament, beads).

Setting up
Make a label from the white paper with 'Made from clay' on and staple it to the display board together with two or three pictures of objects made from clay. Arrange the three cardboard boxes beneath the display board and drape them with the blue fabric. Display four or five objects made from clay on the boxes. Make labels for each one.

What to do
Gather the children around the display and ask them to name each object in turn and describe it in detail to you. Ask the children to use each of their senses (apart from taste) to explore the object. Repeat for the pictures of objects. Draw attention to the fact that each object is made from clay. Suggest the children find objects or pictures of their own to add to the display. As these are brought in, discuss each one in detail.

Questions to ask
What is each object for? What shape, colour and size is it? Does it have any patterns, textures, writing or numbers on it? Is it heavy or light, hard or soft, rough or smooth? Does it smell? What sound does it make if tapped lightly? Is it hot or cold? Will it bend? Look to see if a glaze has been added by comparing the top of the object with the underside. Can you tell what colour the clay is by looking at the base?

For younger children
Choose one object from the display and draw a picture to show it in a context such as a chimney pot on a house or a jug in the kitchen.

For older children
Suggest that older children choose one object from the display and write a list of words to describe it. Display the lists beside each object.

Follow-up activities
● Sort the objects into sets – building materials/crockery/unglazed objects/smooth or patterned objects.
● Compare a dry brick with one submerged in water. Stand another brick in a small amount of water and watch the water rise up the brick.
● Find out about people who work with clay or objects made from clay such as a bricklayer, tilemaker, potter or sculptor.

ZOO TIME

Learning objective
To make a container
from clay.

Group size
Up to six children.

What you need
Dear Zoo by Rod Campbell (Picture Puffin), small plastic zoo/farm animals, wooden baseboards, clay modelling tools (including wire-ended tools), slip, kiln.

Setting up
Read *Dear Zoo* and look closely at the design of the containers used for transporting each different pet. Discuss their shape, size, material and colour. Talk about any writing or numbers on the outside of the containers.

What to do
Allow the children to each choose a small plastic zoo or farm animal and tell them they are going to make a clay container for their animal. Ask each child to roll a piece of clay into a sphere (ball) shape, smoothing any cracks with their fingers. Show them how to shape it into a container shape by tapping the ball of clay gently on the baseboard. Use the wire-ended modelling tools to hollow out the container, keeping the walls and base an even thickness (1cm).

Use the modelling tools to add texture or patterns to the outside of the containers. Discuss whether to cut a window in the side, make a lid or add a handle (using a thick coil and some slip). Allow the finished containers to dry thoroughly and then fire them. If possible, glaze and refire them.

Questions to ask
Remind them that the containers must be suitable for the chosen animals. Does the container need a lid to stop the animal getting out? Would handles make the container easier to carry? Encourage them to place their animals into the container to see if it is suitable. (Remind them to allow a little extra room because the container will shrink slightly when fired.) After firing assess how well they work. Are there any special features which the children particularly like? Display the animals in their finished containers.

For younger children
They may need adult assistance to hollow out their container.

For older children
Give each child some sticky labels and suggest they write signs to stick on the outside of their container.

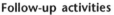

Follow-up activities
● Suggest that each child writes/tells a story about their animal and container.
● Make a collection of boxes. Compare their designs by looking at size, shape, function and materials.
● Mime the *Dear Zoo* story with the children acting as animals.
● Talk about why a dog makes a more suitable pet than a zoo animal. Invite a dog owner to bring their pet to show the children.

BUTTERFLY LIFE CYCLE

Learning objective
To reinforce
understanding of the
life cycle of a butterfly.

Group size
Up to six children.

What you need
The Very Hungry Caterpillar by Eric Carle (Picture Puffin), coloured Plasticine, modelling tools, real leaves, straws, rolling pins, baseboard, six circles of sugar paper, felt-tipped pens.

Setting up
Read the story to the children and use it to introduce the life cycle of a butterfly. Make sure the children know and can sequence the four stages of development – egg, caterpillar, cocoon, butterfly.

What to do
Show each child how to fold a circle of sugar paper into four. Explain that for each quarter, they are going to make Plasticine models for each stage of development in the butterfly life cycle.

The children can either model their own leaves or press real leaves into the Plasticine and then cut them out. Roll small balls of Plasticine into eggs. For caterpillars, roll thick coils of Plasticine and use the modelling tools to add features, patterns and textures. Make more leaves and use a straw to make holes in them. For the cocoons, model an ovoid and use the modelling tools to make indentations. The children may like to hide their cocoons under Plasticine leaves, grass or twigs. For the butterflies, roll a cylinder body shape and pinch out antennae, then roll some Plasticine out flat, cut out wing shapes and make patterns on them by adding different coloured pieces of Plasticine or pressing tools into the surface. The children could make flowers and leaves for their butterflies to sit on.

Place the finished models onto the sugar paper circles and label each quarter appropriately. Display the life cycle circles with the story.

Questions to ask
Encourage the children to name each stage as they make it and ask what stage went before or after. When the models have been placed on the paper circles, ask the children to check each other's models to make sure they are sequenced correctly. Help them realise the cycle is a continuous circle because the adult butterfly lays eggs and so the cycle repeats.

For younger children
Younger children could work as a group and make models for one large life cycle circle. They could also work together to sequence the life cycle.

For older children
Write about the butterfly life cycle and add this work to the display.

Follow-up activities
● Write a story about the adventures of a butterfly (on butterfly shaped paper) and add to the display.
● Print symmetrical patterns on a butterfly-shaped piece of paper. Add the prints to the display.
● Sing 'Tiny Caterpillar', *Bobby Shaftoe, Clap Your Hands* (A & C Black) and 'I'm a Funny Little Caterpillar', *Jumping Jack* (Music Sales Ltd).

SNOWMEN SHAKERS

Learning objective
To observe how
Plasticine reacts with
water.

Group size
Up to six children.

What you need
Coloured Plasticine (including white), modelling tools, baseboard, two sets of six small transparent plastic containers with lids, glitter, water.

Setting up
Give each child a plastic container filled with water and two or three small pieces of different coloured Plasticine. Encourage the children to touch and describe the Plasticine. Put one piece of Plasticine into the water and describe what happens to it. Remove it, feel it again and describe any changes. Try putting different sized and different coloured pieces of Plasticine into the water, and talk about any changes.

What to do
Use the Plasticine to make a snowman or snowlady. Encourage the children to squeeze a head from the body of their piece of Plasticine. Make sure they seal any features, such as eyes, hat, buttons and scarf, well onto the snowman's body. Use the modelling tools to add textures or patterns.

When complete place the snowman onto the upturned lid of the container and seal it well onto the lid. Fill the containers with water and add some glitter. Screw the lid (with the snowman) onto the container. Encourage the children to experiment with their movements to make the glitter move in different ways.

Questions to ask
Ask the children to predict what will happen when the Plasticine snowman is put into the water. Does the glitter float or sink when added to the water? Encourage the children to observe and describe what happens as they move the container. What does the glitter do when you shake the container up and down, or from side to side? Warn the children not to shake the container too hard otherwise the snowman will dislodge!

Follow-up activities
● Experiment with other materials to replace the glitter.
● Put small pieces of clay, play dough and Plasticine into water and compare any changes.
● Collect commercially produced snow scenes. Talk about the materials which have been used to make them.
● Read *The Snow Lady* by Shirley Hughes (Walker Books).

For younger children
An adult may need to help seal the snowmen onto the lids.

For older children
Older children could add more details to their snow scenes such as a Plasticine landscape with trees or bushes.

PICTURE MAPS

Learning objective
To use simple co-
ordinates on a picture
map.

Group size
Up to six children.

What you need
Red, blue and green sugar paper, adhesive, felt-tipped pens, coloured Plasticine, baseboards, modelling tools.

Setting up
Use adhesive tape to join the red, blue and green sugar paper. Draw a large simple grid and label the co-ordinates. Then draw a simple landscape onto the grid.

What to do
Show the children the picture map and identify features in the landscape. Then name the colours and identify the numbers on the grid. Explain that the colours and numbers can help us find out where something is on the map. Show them an example.

Make a tree from Plasticine and place it in one of the rectangles. Help the children read the co-ordinates for that rectangle (such as Green 2). Invite the children to make Plasticine models to place on the picture map. Encourage them to use the modelling tools to add details to their models. Include birds, sun, clouds, aeroplanes, buildings, trees, animals, people, fish and boats. When the children have placed their models on the map, help them practise using the co-ordinates.

Questions to ask
Ask the children to name the co-ordinates for a particular model. Can they list the models in the Blue 1 rectangle? When they can easily identify the co-ordinates, suggest they move a model from one co-ordinate to another. Can they give a similar instruction to a friend?

For younger children
Reduce the number of rectangles on the grid to four, using two colours only.

For older children
Increase the number of rectangles on the grid to nine or even twelve.

Follow-up activities
● Repeat the activity using small world toys on the landscape instead of Plasticine models.
● Give the children a grid on squared paper and suggest they draw their own picture map.
● Encourage the children to make picture maps of a toy farm by drawing round the farm buildings.
● Invite the children to paint road ways on a large piece of paper and use toy vehicles on them.

PHYSICAL DEVELOPMENT

Any work with clay, play dough and Plasticine will aid physical development. Children will improve both their gross and fine motor skills as they handle the materials, tools and equipment themselves. Modelling materials can also inspire and support PE activities.

CLAY DANCE

Learning objective
To use clay to inspire movement.

Group size
Whole class.

What you need
A large open space, tambourine, claves, glockenspiel.

What to do
Tell the children to imagine that they have clay stuck to their fingers. Whenever you shake the tambourine they must pretend to remove the clay by shaking their hands. Travel around the room repeating this. Next they can imagine they are surrounded by sticky mud. Invite them to dip one foot into the mud each time you bang the claves. Repeat with the other foot. Next they can pretend to step into the mud and imagine that they cannot move their feet. As you shake the tambourine, ask the children to do a wobbly dance with the top half of their bodies without moving their feet. Then tell them to pretend to step into a pool of sinking mud. Move the beater on the glockenspiel from high to low as the children sink slowly to the ground and from low to high as the children struggle upwards. Repeat this several times.

Next they can drag themselves through the muddy pool when you shake the tambourine and fall over when you bang it. Explain that the muddy pool is drying up and tap the glockenspiel randomly whilst the children dodge in and out between the remaining muddy puddles. Then occasionally move the beater from low to high as a signal for the children to jump over a muddy puddle. Finish the movement session with all the children miming washing the mud off.

Questions to ask
Remind the children to use the whole available space and not to touch others unless asked to. Suggest that for shaking their hands they try hands together, hands apart, hands high and low. Remind them to move backwards and sideways as well as forwards. In sinking and rising, encourage them to listen carefully and make their movements match the glockenspiel. During the sticky chain tell them to join different parts of their bodies as well as hands.

For younger children
Younger children may benefit from working in a smaller group.

For older children
Invite older children to play the percussion instruments.

Follow-up activities
● Put thin runny clay in a plastic tray for the children to explore with their fingers.
● Write a joint story about an animal who gets stuck in some mud.
● Read the poem 'Puddles' in *Pudmuddle Jump In* (Magnet).

BEADS

Learning objective
To improve control over fine motor movements.

Group size
Up to six children.

What you need
Baseboard, coloured play dough, thin knitting needle, non-stick baking tin, oven, thin elastic (or laces).

What to do
Explain that the children are going to make beads for a necklace or bracelet. Show the children how to make a bead by rolling a small piece of play dough into a sphere on the baseboard and then carefully piercing it with a knitting needle. Show them how to mix two colours by kneading together two different coloured pieces of play dough. Create a marbled effect by partly kneading the dough or make a completely new colour by thorough kneading. Invite the children to use the play dough to make their own beads. When finished, place the beads on the baking tin and bake them in the oven at 150°C (300°F, Gas Mark 2) for three to four hours.

Allow the beads to cool and then make bracelets and necklaces by threading them onto the thin elastic to the required length and then tying the knot.

Questions to ask
Take care when using the knitting needle. Ask the children to name the dough colours before and after kneading. Describe the marbled effect and discuss which two colours produce the best effect. Talk about the shape and size of the beads. Will all the beads be the same size? Can the children make cylinder or cube shaped beads? Compare and contrast the beads before and after baking. How have they changed? When threading the beads, talk about whether the children will cover all the elastic or whether they prefer to leave some showing.

For younger children
Younger children may need adult help to pierce the hole in each bead. They may also find it easier to manipulate larger beads with bigger holes and thicker elastic.

For older children
Older children can make patterns when threading the beads. These may include sequences of shape, size or colour.

Follow-up activities
● Collect necklaces and bracelets made from beads. Compare and contrast the materials, shape, size and patterns used.
● Use plastic and wooden beads to make jewellery for dolls and teddies.
● Practise fine motor control movements on other threading activities such as lacing cards.
● Explore marbling effects in paint by straw-blowing two colours together.
● Look at jewellery from another culture or historical period.

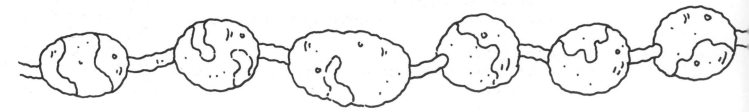

SLAP, BANG, SHAKE!

Learning objective
To explore the effect of hand movements on clay.

Group size
Up to six children.

What you need
Clay, the song 'I can touch', from *Wonderful me!* (Music Sales Limited), hand-shaped pieces of paper, felt-tipped pen, display board covered in green backing paper, stapler, white paper for labels.

Setting up
Learn to sing 'I can touch' and mime the movements to accompany the action words: clap, tap, stroke and pat. Decide which actions could be used on a lump of clay and write each action word on a hand-shaped piece of paper.

What to do
Give each child a lump of clay and try out each action from the song together: tap, stroke, pat, knock, flick and shake the clay. Ask them to describe what effect their actions have on the clay. Can they think of their own actions? These may include slap, bang, squeeze, press, roll, pinch, drop, poke, pull, twist and stretch. As each action is suggested, write each word onto a hand-shaped piece of paper. Test

out all the actions and describe the effects of the clay. At the end of the activity, staple the hand-shaped pieces of paper onto a display board with the title 'I can ...' at the top of the board and '... the clay.' at the bottom.

Questions to ask
Describe the feel of the clay. What marks are created in the clay by the actions? Talk about the differences caused by tapping the clay with the fingers and tapping the whole lump of clay on the table. Listen for sounds as the children slap, drop and bang the clay. What happens if they press different parts of their hand onto the clay? How thin can they roll or pinch a piece of clay? What shapes are produced if the clay is pulled, twisted or stretched? Talk about what the shapes and marks could represent if they were making a model.

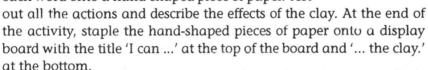

For younger children
Younger children will need an adult to act as scribe for them.

For older children
Older children could use the words in the display to write a simple poem about clay.

Follow-up activities
● Add some hand-shaped models to the display by taking a print of each child's hand in soft clay.
● Ask each child to roll their lump of clay into a snake. Compare and order according to length. Then join all the snakes together to make a giant snake.
● Read the poem 'The Mud Pie Makers Rhyme' in *Twinkle, Twinkle Chocolate Bar* (OUP).

CAR MAZE

Learning objective
To improve hand-eye co-ordination.

Group size
Up to six children.

What you need
Pictures of simple mazes, Plasticine, six large Formica baseboards, six small toy cars.

Setting up
Show and discuss the pictures of mazes. Talk about the different materials used to divide up a maze such as hedges, fences or walls.

What to do
Explain that the children are going to make a maze for a toy car. First ask each child to choose a toy car, give them a baseboard and ask them to use Plasticine to divide up the board to create a maze. Remind them to have a clear entrance and exit. Test to make sure the pathways are large enough for the chosen car to move along. When all the mazes are finished, ask the children to swap and try out each others.

Questions to ask
Talk about designing false trails which lead to dead ends. Use examples in the pictures to inspire ideas. How high will the Plasticine divisions be? Will the divisions be curved or straight? Discuss and evaluate the finished mazes. Which is the hardest/easiest to do? Can the car be moved through the maze without touching any of the divisions? Are there any faults which need to be improved?

For younger children
Make an example of a Plasticine maze for younger children to play with before the activity.

For older children
Ask older children to design their maze first on a piece of paper.

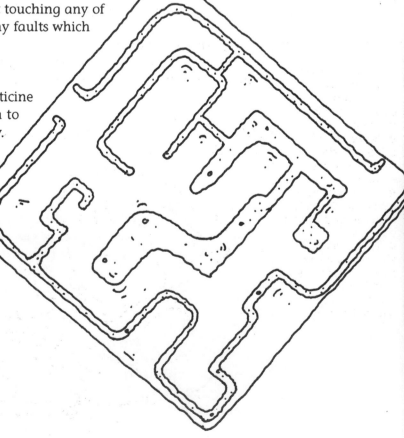

Follow-up activities
● Visit a real maze.
● Chalk a simple maze on a hard surface and invite children to use wheeled vehicles to push or drive through the maze.
● Write a joint story about being lost in a maze.
● Use benches and planks to create raised pathways for children to balance along.
● Read the poem 'Plasticine' in *Twinkle, Twinkle Chocolate Bar* (OUP).

SQUEEZING PLAY DOUGH

Learning objective
To manipulate tools which extrude play dough.

Group size
Up to six children.

What you need
Coloured play dough, baseboards, icing bags/sets, objects with different size and shaped holes, such as a tea strainer, sieve, colander, potato masher or fish slice.

Setting up
Put play dough into the icing bags/sets.

What to do
Invite the children to name and describe the icing bags/sets and objects with holes in. Show them how to use the icing bags/sets and how to push the play dough through the objects with holes in them. Try out the various 'tools' and discuss the effects created.

Questions to ask
Encourage the children to identify that the shape of the play dough is created by being forced through different shaped holes. Can they predict what shape the play dough will be before squeezing it through the holes? Were they correct? Use the icing bags to make curved and straight lines. Count the number of holes in each object. Is it easier to push the play dough through large or small holes? Talk about how the shapes produced could be used when modelling. Could they be used to represent hair or grass for example?

For younger children
Younger children may lack the strength to push the play dough through fine holes so choose objects with large holes.

For older children
Older children could make a picture with the shapes produced by extruding.

Follow-up activities
● Invite the children to find their own objects with holes in (in the room or at home) and test them out.
● Experiment with commercially-produced play dough extruding machines.
● Make models using play dough shapes produced by extruding.
● Make biscuits or cakes and decorate them using the icing bags/sets.
● Collect and talk about pictures of special cakes (such as wedding or christening) with decorative icing.

COPY-CAT STATUES

Learning objective
To observe and copy body shapes.

Group size
Whole class.

What you need
A large space.

Setting up
The children will need to have had some experience of using play dough.

What to do
Ask the children to stand in a circle. Choose one child to stand in the middle and to pretend to be a lump of play dough. Choose a child from the circle to move the first child into a statue shape. Invite the children in the circle to copy the pose of the finished statue and to hold it without moving for a short time. The child who created the statue becomes the next 'lump of play dough' and chooses another child from the circle to create a new statue. Repeat the activity as often as desired.

Follow-up activities
● Look at statues in gardens, garden centres and art galleries. Describe and copy their shapes.
● Make simple figures from play dough and try out different poses.
● Watch animated films with characters made from modelling materials. Talk about the movements made by one of the characters in a short sequence.

Questions to ask
Remind the child in the middle that play dough would be floppy and easy to move. Name the body parts being moved and encourage the children to think of less obvious poses such as kneeling or lying down. Reinforce positional vocabulary by asking the children to describe the location of various limbs. Are both hands in the same position? Are the feet together or apart? Which parts of the body are high? Which parts of the body are supporting the weight? Talk about how easy or difficult it is to copy the statue shape exactly. Is it harder to keep still with some shapes than others?

For younger children
Younger children may benefit from working in a smaller group.

For older children
Use a one-minute sand timer to measure the time for holding the pose.

PANCAKE RACE

Learning objective
To improve control of gross motor movements.

Group size
Up to eight children.

What you need
Large grassed area, two long pieces of tape, four frying pans, four lumps of Plasticine.

Setting up
Mark a start and finish line on the grass with the two pieces of tape.

What to do
Ask the children to get into pairs. Give each pair a frying pan and invite them to make a pancake from a lump of Plasticine.

Practise walking and then running holding the frying pans and pancakes. Point out the start and finishing line, and ask one child from each pair to stand at the start line holding the frying pan. Their partners should stand half-way along the track.

Explain that the children at the start line are going to run along the track trying not to drop their pancake. When they reach their partner, they hand over the frying pan and the second child completes the race to the finishing tape. The winning team is the first to cross the finishing line with their frying pan and pancake. If a child drops a pancake during the race, they can stop and pick it up.

Questions to ask
Talk about finding an appropriate speed for the race. What happens if you run too fast or too slow? Is there a more comfortable way of holding the frying pan? How can they stop the pancake from slipping off the frying pan? What is the best way of handing over the frying pan from one partner to another?

For younger children
Younger children could run a shorter distance and work individually.

For older children
Older children could run a longer distance. They could also climb over obstacles or toss the pancake at the end of the race.

Follow-up activities
● Find out about Pancake Day and why we celebrate it.
● Make sweet and savoury pancakes.
● Read the story *The Big Pancake* from the Well Loved Tales Series (Ladybird).
● Learn the rhyme 'Mix a pancake' in *This Little Puffin* (Young Puffin).

WHEELS

Learning objective
To manipulate tools
used for rolling
textures.

Group size
Up to six children.

What you need
Coloured play dough, baseboard, rolling pins, a selection of rollers such as wheels from construction kits, toy cars with textured tyres, lids with serrated edges, commercially-produced textured rollers, wheeled pastry cutters.

What to do
Give each child a piece of play dough and a baseboard. Ask them to roll their play dough out on the baseboard. Then show them how to use the selection of rollers to press textures in their play dough. Invite them to experiment with the different rollers. Discuss the different effects achieved.

Questions to ask
Encourage the children to feel the texture on each roller and then feel the texture it creates in the play dough. Talk about the differences achieved by pressing lightly or firmly. Encourage them to experiment with the type of lines produced. Can they make straight, curved or spiral lines? What effect is produced if the lines are placed side by side or overlapped? How could these effects be used when making a picture or model?

For younger children
Improve younger children's control by drawing a line on their play dough and asking them to roll on top of it.

For older children
Older children can make their own rollers by sticking string or textured wallpaper onto cardboard tubes.

Follow-up activities
● Make pictures or models using rollers in play dough.
● Invite the children to find their own wheels for rolling and test them out.
● Collect toy vehicles and match pairs according to tyre prints.
● Test the rollers out in a different material such as Plasticine, damp sand, paint or water.
● Sing 'Wheels keep turning' from *Apusskidu* (A & C Black).

CHAPTER SIX

Materials such as clay, play dough and Plasticine have obvious value in creative art and design work. However musical activities can also be developed using these materials. Both areas develop children's abilities to express ideas and feelings and to use their imagination.

COLOUR MATCHING

Learning objective
To match Plasticine to pictures by colour.

Group size
Up to six children.

What you need
Six copies of photocopiable activity sheet on page 64, felt-tipped pens, six plastic wallets, coloured Plasticine, modelling tools.

Setting up
Colour in each flower on the activity sheet a different colour using the felt-tipped pens. Make each activity sheet different, and then place each sheet into a plastic wallet.

What to do
Hand out the activity sheets to the children and ask them to make a butterfly to match the colour of each flower using Plasticine. To make a butterfly, tell the children to roll a cylinder shaped body and pinch out two antennae. Shape some wings and fix them firmly to the body. Match up the finished butterflies and flowers and talk about what they have achieved. Swap sheets to repeat the activity.

Questions to ask
As the children work, encourage them to name the colour of the flowers and butterflies. When all the sheets are completed, count the number of red or blue flowers. Muddle up the butterflies and see how quickly the children can match them to their correct flower. Misplace one or two butterflies on each sheet and ask the children to spot the mistakes.

For younger children
Younger children could use a butterfly-shaped pastry cutter.

For older children
Invite older children to make more elaborate butterflies by using the modelling tools to impress patterns on the wings. They could also match the colour words (written on small pieces of card shaped like flower pots) to each flower.

Follow-up activities
● Paint a vase of flowers using shades of one colour.
● Talk about Vincent Van Gogh's *Sunflowers* painting.
● Play colour pairs, where the children work in pairs, with one child using pastry cutters to make Plasticine shapes in different colours. The second child has to make a second set which matches the first in both colour and shape.
● Make coloured jellies and match the correct coloured plastic spoon to each one.

FLOWER POT BELLS

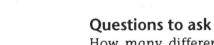

Learning objective
To explore sounds made by tapping clay flower pots.

Group size
Up to six children.

What you need
Six clay flower pots (different sizes), a plastic flower pot, paints, paintbrushes, palettes, seven large wooden beads, seven pieces of string, wooden pole, a selection of beaters made from different materials (such as hard and soft musical beaters, a metal spoon, thick/thin pieces of wood, paintbrush, cardboard tube, plastic ruler).

Setting up
Ask the children to describe the clay flower pots, noting their shape, size, colour and texture. Compare the plastic flower pot with the clay ones.

What to do
Explain that the children are going to use the flower pots as bells but first they are going to decorate them. Give each child a clay flower pot and turn it upside down. Invite them to use the paints to decorate the outside of the flower pot, using patterns (spots, stripes, zigzags) or pictures (flowers, insects). Allow the paint to dry and then thread and tie a bead onto each string. Push the string through the hole in the base of each flower pot and suspend it by attaching it to the wooden pole. Also hang up the plastic flower pot.

Use the beaters to create as many different sounds as possible. Then find other objects in the room to use as beaters. Warn the children not to use excessive force when tapping the flower pots.

Questions to ask
How many different sounds can be made by one beater? Does it make the same sounds on all the flower pots? Do both ends of the beater make the same sound? Does it make any difference if you tap the top, the side or the rim of the flower pot? Compare tapping lightly, strongly, slowly and quickly. Which beater produces their favourite sound?

For younger children
Help younger children suspend their flower pots.

For older children
Invite older children to use the flower pot bells to compose a short piece of music to play to the rest of the group.

Follow-up activities
● Suggest that the children collect and suspend other objects to tap. Compare the resulting sound with the flower pots.
● Introduce the children to percussion instruments which can be tapped such as tambour, triangle and cymbal.
● Place a set of flower pots in order according to size.
● Use plastic flower pots as construction toys. What can the children build with them?

COLOUR MIXING

Learning objective
To examine the effect of mixing two primary colours.

Group size
Up to six children.

What you need
Cornflour, water, red, yellow and blue food colouring, scales, measuring jug, three bowls, three large spoons, six shallow containers (such as sponge-baking tins, plastic drip trays for flower pots), modelling tools and forks.

Setting up
Let the children help you make up the cornflour mixture (if there is time). This is a thin cornflour play dough mix which has some very interesting properties. Place 175g cornflour, 250ml water and some red food colouring into a bowl. Mix together thoroughly with a spoon. Repeat in separate bowls with the other two primary colours. Talk with the children about the characteristics of each ingredient and any changes that have happened.

What to do
Give each child a shallow container and ask them to spoon into it some of the mixture from one colour. Stir the colours well each time before spooning them out. Then ask the children to choose another colour and spoon some of that into their container. Initially they can mix the two colours with their fingers and then try the modelling tools and forks. Compare the results and discuss any differences.

Questions to ask
Talk about the texture of the cornflour mixture and ask the children to describe how it feels. Does it stick to their fingers or run off? Can they predict what colour will be produced when red and yellow are mixed together? How many different colours can they see in their container? Does mixing blue and yellow always produce a shade of green? What happens when they drag a fork across several colours?

For younger children
Younger children could mix the colours with their fingers only.

For older children
Suggest the children predict what will happen if the mixture is allowed to dry. Compare their predictions with what actually happens.

HICKORY DICKORY

Learning objective
To make a model to
accompany a nursery
rhyme.

Group size
Up to six children.

What you need
'Hickory Dickory Dock' from, *Sing Hey Diddle Diddle* (A & C Black), pictures of mice and clocks, plain play dough, dough paste, brush for paste, baseboard, modelling tools, non-stick baking tray, oven, wool, PVA adhesive/sticks, small cardboard boxes, paints, paintbrushes, palettes, white paper, clock stamp and pad, card, scissors, six split pins.

Setting up
Learn to sing Hickory Dickory Dock with accompanying actions together. Look at the pictures of mice and discuss their physical characteristics. Show the children the pictures of clocks and talk about the different types. Print up some clock faces onto sheets of paper ready for use.

What to do
Make a play dough mouse to accompany the rhyme. Ask each child to roll and pat a piece of play dough into an ovoid (egg) shape on their baseboard. Smooth any cracks with their fingers. Squeeze out a head shape from one end, pinch out two ears and then use the modelling tools to add eyes, nose and mouth. Squeeze out four short sturdy legs and scratch a 'furry' texture all over the body. Place the finished models on the baking tray and bake at 150°C (Gas mark 2, 300°F) for three to four hours. When cool, stick a wool tail onto each mouse. Allow the children to choose the colour and length of their tail.

Next make a clock for each mouse. Turn a cardboard box inside out and reassemble it, paint and decorate it. When dry, stick a clock face sheet on the front of the box. Cut two card hands and use the split pin to fix them to the clock face. Ask each child to use their mouse and clock to join in when singing the rhyme.

Questions to ask
Refer the children back to the pictures of mice for ideas on their physical characteristics. Count the number of legs and eyes. Which modelling tool produces the best fur texture? How has the play dough changed after baking? Use the pictures of clocks for inspiration for making cardboard clocks.

For younger children
Younger children will need help to turn their cardboard boxes inside out and to insert the split pins.

For older children
Older children can paint their play dough mouse after it has been baked.

Follow-up activities
● Sort the mice into sets according to colour or length of tail.
● Arrange for someone to bring in a pet mouse.
● Collect and display different types of clock.
● Play 'What's the time Mr Wolf?'.
● Listen to music with a clock theme such as 'The Syncopated Clock' by Leroy Anderson or Haydn's London Symphony.

PRINTING WALLPAPER

Learning objective
To make Plasticine
blocks for printing
wallpaper.

Group size
Up to six children.

What you need
Samples of wallpaper, old Plasticine, baseboards, modelling
tools, objects to press into the Plasticine (such as metal nuts,
comb, different shaped lids, Duplo, shells, dried poppy
heads), coloured printing inks, shallow tray with sponge
pad for each colour, long strips of paper, scissors.

Setting up
Show and discuss the samples of wallpaper with the
children. Talk about the colours, shapes and pictures used
in the decoration. Identify any repeats in the patterns. Suggest the
children make some wallpaper for the home corner (for example).
Decide which walls are to be papered and cut out the long strips of
paper to the right length.

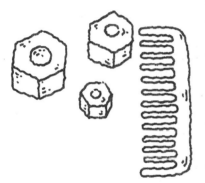

What to do
To make a printing block, ask each child to shape a lump of
Plasticine into a cube or cuboid by tapping it lightly on the
baseboard. Then use the modelling tools and the other objects
to press shapes and patterns into the base of their block.
When complete show the children how to press it gently into
the printing ink. Make a print on one of the strips of paper
by pressing the inked block gently up and down. Remind
them not to drag the block sideways otherwise the print will
be smudged. Allow the children to work in pairs on one strip
of paper, using their block and one colour each to print.

Questions to ask
What impressions are created by the different modelling
tools and objects. Remind the children to smooth out any
unsatisfactory marks in their Plasticine block with their
fingers. Talk about the print created by their block. Will
they print randomly over the paper or will they organise a
repeating pattern? Do they want to overlap two colours?
Assess the finished wallpaper and discuss how any faults
could be rectified. Are there prints where too much or too
little ink has been used?

Follow-up activities
● Play pairs by
matching wallpaper
samples.
● Use textured
wallpaper samples
for taking wax
rubbings.
● Use wallpaper
samples for a collage
picture.
● Ask children to
describe in detail the
wallpaper in their
bedroom. Invite
them to give reasons
for liking/disliking it.
● Visit a DIY shop
with a range of
wallpapers.

For younger children
Younger children may need help making the Plasticine into a cube/
cuboid shape. They are also more likely to produce a random pattern.

For older children
Older children could work individually, making two blocks each.
Encourage them to show repeating patterns on their wallpaper. They
may also like to make borders to go round the top or across the middle
of their paper.

SHAKERS

Learning objective
To explore sounds by
making shakers.

Group size
Up to six children.

What you need

A collection of shakers with different materials inside, coloured play dough, baseboards, non-stick baking tray, oven, six containers with lids (either totally transparent such as juice bottles or partly transparent such as a cream pot with a transparent lid). Try to choose containers made from different materials such as cardboard or tin.

Setting up

Allow the children to play with the shakers and then discuss each one. Talk about the sounds they produce and the materials used for the container and the beans inside.

What to do

Tell the children they are going to make their own beans for a shaker. Give each child a baseboard and ask them to choose two small pieces of different coloured play dough. Suggest they knead the two colours together. Then pinch off small pieces of the kneaded dough and roll them into spheres (ball shapes). Place the spheres on the baking sheet and bake at 150°C (300°F, Gas mark 2) for three to four hours.

When cool, the children can place their beans inside a container of their choice. Test out each shaker to discover how many different sounds it can produce. Vary the size of beans placed in the container.

Questions to ask

Talk about what happens when two different coloured play doughs are kneaded together. Encourage the children to make spheres in different sizes. Compare the spheres before and after baking and discuss any changes. Talk about which beans the children are going to use in their container. Watch the beans move as they shake them. Is a different sound produced if the beans are shaken from side to side compared with up and down? Do large and small beans produce the same sound? Also compare containers made from different materials.

For younger children

Simplify the activity by making the beans all the same size.

For older children

Vary the number of beans and compare the sounds produced. Do lots of beans together make a different sound to a few?

MAKING MONSTERS

Learning objective
To combine play dough and reclaimed materials to create imaginary monsters.

Group size
Up to six children.

What you need
Where the Wild Things Are by Maurice Sendak (Picture Lions), coloured play dough, dough paste, paintbrush for paste, baseboard, modelling tools, a selection of reclaimed materials; for example natural materials such as twigs, leaves, fir cones, small pebbles, shells and man-made materials such as coloured matchsticks, pipe-cleaners, coloured paper clips and string.

Setting up
Read *Where the Wild Things Are* and talk about the monsters in the illustrations. Describe their physical characteristics and focus on any patterns and textures.

What to do
Explain that the children are going to make their own imaginary monsters. Suggest they use play dough to form the body and the head. Remind them of basic techniques such as pinching and squeezing legs and tails from the play dough. Also make sure they remember to use dough paste if they are going to add features. Use the reclaimed materials to represent ears, horns, wings or tails. Make sure these are firmly embedded in the play dough. Suggest they use the modelling tools to add textures or patterns to their monsters. Allow the monsters to air dry.

Questions to ask
Refer the children to the illustrations in the story for ideas. Talk about the different kinds of body parts the children might like to include on their monsters. Will it have antennae, spines or claws? Which reclaimed materials will best represent these? Is the body of the monster rough or smooth? Which modelling tool will create a suitable texture? Talk about any changes in the play dough as it dries. Evaluate the finished monsters. Which do the children like best and why? Select one of the reclaimed materials and look to see how many different ways it has been used on the models.

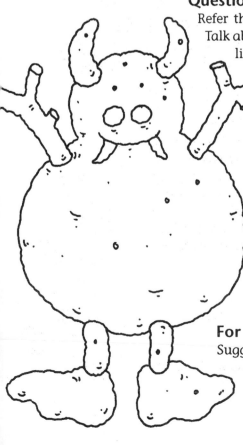

For younger children
Encourage younger children to use the reclaimed items to add features to their monsters rather than using play dough and paste.

For older children
Suggest older children make an environment for their monster using their own choice of materials.

Follow-up activities
● Sort the reclaimed materials into two sets – natural and man-made.
● Invent a name for each monster, write it on paper and stick reclaimed materials over each letter.
● Make up a group story about one of the monsters.
● Read *The Monster Bed* by Jeanne Willis and Sue Varley (Beaver Books).

HOLES

Learning objective
To learn how to carve into a piece of clay.

Group size
Up to six children.

What you need
A collection of objects with holes (natural such as stones, wood, nut shells and man-made such as graters, colanders and nets), clay, wooden baseboard, modelling tools (including wire ended).

Setting up
Show and discuss the collection of objects with holes. Talk about the size, shape and pattern of the holes.

What to do
Ask each child to roll, tap and pat a piece of clay into a shape of their choice. Invite them to use the modelling tools to cut or press holes into their shape. Remind them to leave enough clay so that the shape still supports itself. Allow the finished sculptures to dry and then display them with the objects which inspired them.

Questions to ask
Talk about the initial shape the children make. Is it regular such as a sphere or cube? Will the holes be pressed into the surface, penetrate half-way or all the way through the shape? Do the children want the edge of their holes to be smooth or rough? Remind them to view their clay shape from different angles.

For younger children
Younger children may need an adult to work through an example with them first.

For older children
Encourage older children to try making some of the supporting structures as thin as possible without losing any strength in the sculpture.

Follow-up activities
● Look at sculptures with holes in them.
● Sort plastic or wooden letters into sets – those with holes in them and those without.
● Set up large apparatus with a holes theme by using hoops, tunnels and cardboard boxes.
● Use objects with holes in the sand. Try sieves, funnels, colanders and pipes.
● Collect and discuss food with holes such as cheese, sponge and pasta.

PHOTOCOPIABLES

Name _____

Name _____

Throw the dice and colour one matching shape.

Name _____

Name _____

Colour a different pattern on each snake.

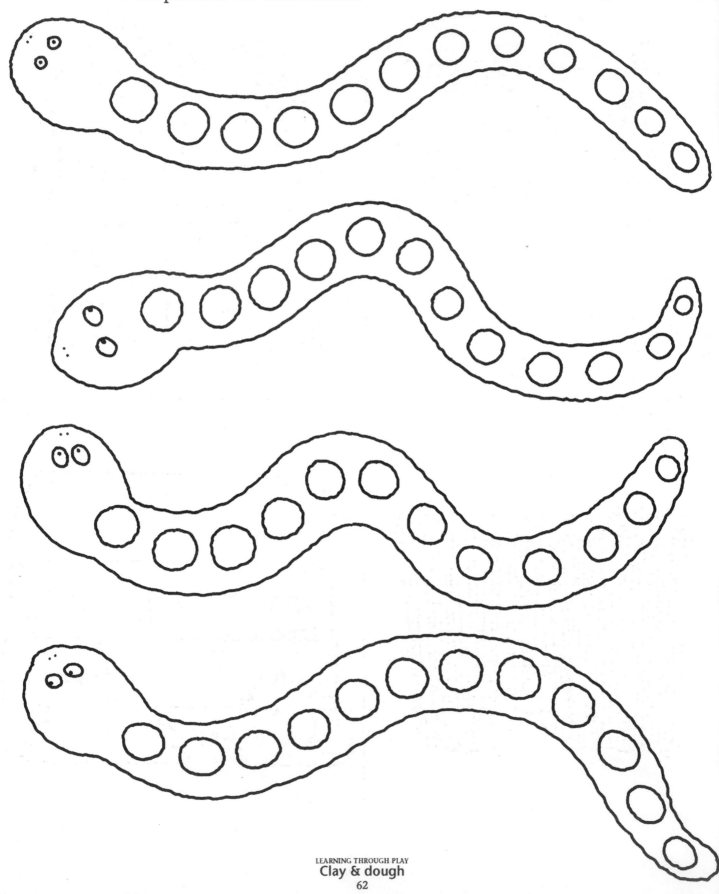

Name _____

Colour the fox.

Name _____

Make a butterfly to match the colour of each flower.

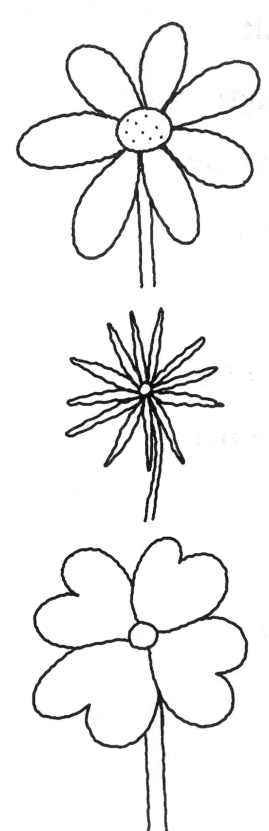